Western Christianity has been willingly hypnotized into a pre-Reformational state becoming religiously ecumenical and morally bankrupt. Simply put, we are in need of a new Reformation mindset which recaptures the tenets of the Reformers of the sixteenth and seventeenth centuries. The re-release of Carl Trueman's *Reformation: Yesterday, Today and Tomorrow* is a needed corrective and powerful antidote for the spiritual anemia that has infected our chapter of church history. It is historically compelling, wonderfully practical, and spiritually motivating.

Rick Holland
Senior Pastor,
Mission Road Bible Church, Kansas City, Kansas

The present has inextricable links to the past. This is obvious, though possibly not to some moderns who think themselves wiser than reality. Trueman is thankfully not one of these moderns and, drawing upon a rich fund of knowledge of the Reformation, he here shows that the Reformation is not at all over but has ongoing relevance. A great introduction to the present-day meaning of this world-changing event.

Michael Haykin
Professor of Church History and Biblical Spirituality,
The Southern Baptist Theological Seminary, Louisville, Kentucky
and
Director of *The Andrew Fuller Center for Baptist Studies*

This fine book should be required reading for all Christians—and especially for those who doubt whether the Protestant Reformation has anything left to say to us in our day. Stating that "the Reformation represents a move to place God as he has revealed himself in Christ at the centre of the church's life and thought," Trueman then retrieves Luther's theology of the cross, argues that because the Reformation "was above all a movement of the Word—incarnate in Christ and written down in th

D0828033

the Spirit works through the Word, "the Word written and the Word preached are both central to Christianity and are not simply cultural forms which can be shed when culture moves on," and then closes with a chapter on Christian assurance that recognizes our assurance as the foundation for our Christian activity. Along the way, he scatters nugget after nugget of insight into what is core to the Reformation legacy, motivating his readers to embrace this core again.

Mark R. Talbot
Associate Professor of Philosophy,
Wheaton College, Wheaton, Illinois

With knowledge, wit, and clarity, Carl Trueman brings key insights from the Reformation on Christ, Scripture, and our appropriation of both to bear on the life of the modern evangelical church. This is not antiquarian theology. Rather we're given a sharp diagnosis of our current shallow experience of God, and prescribed instead the rich, deep, satisfying currents of Biblical Christianity. This little volume will repay both the minster and the layman's repeated reading. I am so glad to see it back in print.

Michael Lawrence
Senior Pastor,
Hinson Baptist Church, Portland, Oregon

Dr Trueman calls us to build on the work of Reformers by a continuing reformation of the church under the Word; especially with regard to the cross of the Christ, the written and preached Word, and thirdly, the assurance of salvation... I commend them to a wider Christian public for reflection, prayer and appropriate reforming action.

Eryl Davies,
Head of Research,
Wales Evangelical School of Theology, Bridgend, Wales

RE-FORM-ATION:

YESTERDAY, TODAY AND TOMORROW

CARL TRUEMAN

CHRISTIAN
FOCUS

Copyright © Carl Trueman 2000

ISBN 978-1-84550-701-5

10 9 8 7 6 5 4 3 2 1

First published in 2000 with Bryntirion Press
Reprinted in 2011 & 2012
by
Christian Focus Publications,
Geanies House, Fearn,
Ross-shire, IV20 1TW, Scotland
www.christianfocus.com
with
Bryntirion Press
Pen-y-bont ar Ogwr/Bridgend
CF31 4DX, Wales, Great Britain

Cover design by Moose77.com

Printed in the USA

CONTENTS

ACKNOWLEDGMENTS

I would like to thank the staff at the Evangelical Theological College of Wales, and particularly its Principal, Dr D Eryl Davies, both for the opportunity of delivering these lectures at the Word and Spirit Conference in July 2000, and for friendship over the years. I am also grateful to Bryntirion Press for their willingness to publish them. I would also like to thank Willie Mackenzie for suggesting a second edition, and to all the folk at Christian Focus for making this possible.

I would like to dedicate these lectures to Arthur S Johnson, English eccentric.

Carl R. Trueman
Newburgh
March 2011

FORE-WORD

One of the drawbacks of putting one's thoughts into print is that it is then so much easier for others to hold one to account for them. Thus, the wise author will not always be disappointed that a book, particularly a book written in comparative youth, goes out of print. The thoughts such a book contains may have been published; but languishing on the shelf in some library, they are a little less likely to haunt the writer's nightmares than otherwise.

It was thus with some trepidation that I greeted the request from Christian Focus to reprint my little, and long-forgotten, book on the contemporary relevance of some aspects of Reformation theology. I had written the book in haste in 1999, in order to deliver at a conference at the Evangelical theological College in Wales. When I did so, I had not yet reached the age of forty, that somewhat arbitrary boundary marker, on the far side of which it is acceptable, and indeed expected, that one will become dyed in the wool, set in one's ways and inflexible in thought. Thus, I did wonder if, in the intervening years, I might have changed my mind in fundamental ways on the matters about which I had chosen to opine.

It was with some relief, therefore, that I find that, upon a review of the book, I am still in substantial agreement with much that I said all those years ago. I still believe that a critical appropriation of the Reformation is vital to a healthy church today. I am now perhaps more concerned than ever about the need for the church to give her people a realistic view of what cross-centred Christian life and experience are. I am persuaded that the doctrine of scripture, both in terms of the phenomenon of scripture and its function in the church, will remain a primary battleground within the church. Finally, given the lure of Roman Catholicism for many disillusioned evangelicals, I believe that a proper emphasis on biblical assurance is not only necessary for a healthy Christian life but is perhaps more polemically significant now than at any time since the Reformation.

Of course, were I to write the book today, it would be different in certain respects. I would most certainly include a chapter on the importance of creeds and confessions for the effective communication, inculcation and preservation of the faith from place to place and generation to generation. I would also add a chapter on the importance of a clear understanding of the importance of the visible church and of the communion of saints, given that these vital aspects of New Testament Christianity have become so weak in our culture of consumerism and virtual reality. Finally, I would want to modify, or at least off-set, my promotion of biblical theological teaching and preaching by emphasizing the need for the preacher to confront and engage his hearers. `Hey, I bet you never saw Jesus in this text before,' is not an adequate application of the Bible; and yet too many so-called redemptive historical preachers and teachers in the Vos (or perhaps, to be charitable and not to impute the sins of the followers to the founder) pseudo-Vos tradition, consider their job to be done when they produced a nice, neat, dry-as-dust lecture on a passage which does just that and no more.

In conclusion, I have always been delighted and somewhat surprised at the positive notes of gratitude and encouragement I received as a result of the first edition of this little book; and I trust this new edition will also prove helpful in some small way to a new generation of readers.

Carl R. Trueman
Westminster Theological Seminary
January 2011

1 THE PEARL OF GREAT PRICE

The Relevance of the Reformation today

To some, the idea that the Reformation of the sixteenth and seventeenth centuries could have anything to teach the church of today would be regarded as nonsense. After all, the sixteenth century happened four hundred years ago. Since then, we have witnessed the birth and death of modernity, the rise and fall of empires, the rapid secularisation of society, the decline of great parts of the West, and the increasing cultural dominance of science and the television. What can some cluster of events from three to four hundred years ago which took place in societies dominated by white European males possibly teach us today, living as we do in the age of mass communication, cosmopolitanism and advanced consumerism? Surely these things are irrelevant?

In addition to this, we live in times when the answer to contemporary problems is always seen to lie in the new and the different. Whether the cause of this constant need for novelty is that consumerism which always needs more and is never satisfied with what it has, or is the result of the impact of ideas of progress and evolution, whereby the best is always yet to come, the result is clear: the past is simply not looked upon as a source of wisdom or guidance for the present and the future. The ubiquity of the epithet 'post-' added on to everything, from postmodernism to postevangelicalism, is symptomatic of this tendency, as is the rhetoric used of those who are always seeking to break with past ways of doing things: they are the radicals, the visionaries, the risk takers. Those who defend any aspect of tradition, whether in belief or practice, are likely to find themselves tarred with the brush of reaction, bigotry, thoughtlessness and fear. The idea that new is good and old is bad runs deep in contemporary society, and this affects the evangelical church as well as the wider culture. The underlying assumption in many quarters is that the past is of no use to the church in the present. We need to bring in new management, repackage ourselves in a more attractive wrapper, and market ourselves in a slicker fashion.

RESCUING THE REFORMATION

I hope that in what follows I am able to persuade at least some who might consider some sympathy with such a position that the past is perhaps not as irrelevant as we might be tempted to feel. I want to argue that key insights of the Reformers are as relevant today—and as applicable to situations to-day—as they were in the sixteenth century.

Unhelpful friends

But my intention is not simply to rescue the Reformation from its detractors; it also needs to be rescued from some of its friends. There is a brand of Christian for whom the fact that 'it'—whether an aspect of practice, a form of words, a particular doctrine—was held by the Reformers is a straightforward knock down argument for saying that 'it' is right for today. We all know such people. They are often those who have reacted (and rightly reacted) against the marginalising of the Reformers in church life which has been going on now for decades. The dominant role taken by the ecumenical movement throughout a large period of the twentieth century undoubtedly played a part in this. The Reformation was, after all, the time when the western church split right down the middle, Protestants and Catholics, and then fragmented some more, as Protestantism divided into Lutheran and Reformed. Such a tragic period in church history was, from the ecumenical viewpoint, something which needed to be dealt with in order to re-establish unity; and so it was dealt with at various times by regarding the theological disputes as either misplaced from the outset or of no contemporary relevance.

Against such a background, it was right and proper that many chose to take a firm stand. It is indeed still right to assert the central significance of an issue such as justification by grace through faith, and to portray attempts to undermine this in any way as necessarily involving changes of fundamental theological significance in how Christianity and its history is to be understood. Nevertheless, I suspect that for many of this group, as they reacted against the ecumenical agenda, the Reformers and the Reformation came to hold the status of supreme icons or authorities, whereby any questioning or criticism of them was viewed as tantamount to heresy.

In addition, the agenda of reaction was always doomed ultimately to be the agenda set by the ecumenists: if justification formed a central focus of the ecumenical attack, so it formed a central part of the conservative defence; and the result was that the emphases and concerns of the Reformers themselves and of the Reformation as a whole came to be read through the lens of debates that were going on within the twentieth-century church. This was not necessarily a bad thing; but it was somewhat restricting. If the Reformers had things to teach outside the immediate debates generated by ecumenism, how were we to see it when the questions we brought to the great texts of Reformation theology said as much about church politics in our century as about anything that had gone on in the sixteenth? Other issues of central importance, such as assurance, the sacraments and the person and work of Christ, were only discussed along the narrow lines determined by the ecumenical movement, and much of value was thereby lost.

An identity crisis

My task here, then, is not to disparage those who have defended the Reformation heritage so valiantly over the last fifty years. We should be grateful to them, particularly at the present time when evangelicalism seems less sure of its identity than at any point in its history. I never cease to be shocked by how little I have in common with many others in the United Kingdom who now claim the name evangelical. One can deny that God knows the future, one can deny that the Bible is inspired, one can deny that justification is by grace through faith, one can deny that Christ is the only way to salvation—one can do all of these things and still remain a member in good standing of certain high-profile evangelical bodies.

The confusion such a situation represents indicates both the doctrinal and, perhaps more importantly, the moral void that lies at the heart of so much British evangelicalism at this time, when few if any are willing to take the difficult decision to stand firm on the non-negotiable aspects of the faith. We desperately need a deeper grasp of the importance of these issues if we are not to sell our heritage for a pot of stew.

A biblical agenda

Nevertheless, we should not let the heterodox, the heretical and downright blasphemous positions of the various cuckoos in our evangelical nest set the agenda. Instead, I would argue that we must allow our agenda to be set by biblical priorities. For that reason, I want in these chapters to broaden the discussion, to come to the Reformation with fresh eyes, looking not just for evidence that, say, justification by grace through faith was a very important doctrine and was indeed repudiated by the Catholic Church, but also to seek out other lessons which may be learned from this most important of periods in church history.

DEFINING THE REFORMATION

Our first task is therefore to produce a working definition of the Reformation which will serve as a formative guide for what is to follow. Now, this is, of course, impossible in an absolute, final and definitive sense since the Reformation embodies so many elements—theological, political, social, cultural and economic—and none of these elements is entirely separable from any of the others, if for no other reason than that real life does not break down into neat, discrete categories. What I wish to do is somewhat more modest, that is, to offer a definition of the Reformation in terms of its broad theological contribution to the thought of the church. I hope thereby to open up avenues of theological reflection which the various popular stereotypes of Reformation thought have missed. By doing so, I trust that I will provoke the reader to think about how the principles of the Reformation might be applied today in a manner which neither misses their timeless theological import, nor simply indulges in a mindless doctrinal reductionis.

The broad definition I propose is as follows: the Reformation represents a move to place God as he has revealed himself in Christ at the centre of the church's life and thought. In subsequent chapters, I will expand upon three particular aspects of this: the church's emphasis upon Jesus Christ and him crucified; the emphasis upon Scripture as the basis and norm for the proclamation of Christ; and the church's accent on assurance of salvation as the normative experience for all Christian believers.

Parameters

In expounding on the theme of the Reformation in general, and on these three themes in particular, I want to make it quite clear from the outset that I am specifically not trying to do two things which some may perhaps be expecting me to do. First, I am in no way providing a text which will bypass the need for reading the Reformers first hand. Their thought is so vast, rich, and complex that it cannot even begin to be summarised, let alone expounded in any depth, in four brief chapters. You must read them for yourselves if you wish to mine from them the nuggets of theological gold which their vast writings contain. These texts are not obscure, and they are easily available today. I would suggest that, just as the Reformers read the works of the medievals and the early church Fathers in order to sharpen their own understanding of the Bible and of Christian tradition, ministers and thoughtful lay people should today read the Reformers. From the exhilarating and fiery prose of Luther to the cooler, more thoughtful writings of Calvin, there is much in the vast literary output of these men that is both theologically useful and devotionally humbling. They are in many ways good models of learning and commitment, and are worth studying for these things, particularly in the present day when the temptation to regard ministers as the godly equivalent of social workers can be so strong.

Second, I am not trying to make the case that we should simply go back to the sixteenth and seventeenth centuries, see what was done then, and bring those practices straight to the present day as if such a move were straightforward. All Christian practice is shaped by the time in which it occurs, and it would be naive not to acknowledge that fact at the outset. I am interested in the theological principles underlying the Reformers' work and in understanding how those principles might be applied in practice today, given that God has not changed, our theology has not changed, but certain aspects of our culture and society have changed. In this, I confess my debt to the men of the Sydney Diocese and Moore College who have sought for many years to bring Reformation insights to bear upon the modern church in the modern world. These chapters are intended as my own tiny contribution to a project which is, I believe, of pressing importance in the present cultural atmosphere of consumerism and eclecticism. To stress the value of Reformation thought today without giving due weight to the difference between the society of the sixteenth century and our own will have the result of unwittingly condemning the Reformers to irrelevance of persuading our postevangelical gurus of the wisdom of their own position. We need to make sure that our defence of the Reformers does not merely demonstrate how outmoded and useless they are.

Theology the driving force

To return to my working definition of the Reformation then: the Reformation represents a move to place God as he has revealed himself in Christ at the centre of the church's life and thought. This is extremely important because we must remember first and foremost that, if the Reformation is a significant moment in church history, and if the Reformers are significant theologians for us today, it is only to the extent that they represent faithful attempts to place God in Christ at the centre. It is beyond dispute that many Reformers were brave men; that they achieved many great things; that they attacked many manifest theological, ecclesiastical and moral abuses; and that some of them died terrible deaths for their beliefs. Yet none of these things, either individually or taken together, means that they have anything to teach us today. Many non-Christians have been brave; many have achieved wonderful things; many have spoken out against abuses; and many have died heroic and steadfast deaths for their beliefs. But, as the old saying goes, a good death does not sanctify a bad cause. Moreover, none of the other actions listed makes any individual of perennial relevance to the church. It is only to the extent that they brought God and Christ to bear upon the church of their day that the Reformers have any ongoing relevance for us today.

Luther himself hinted at this when he described the difference between himself and his precursors, John Wyclif and John Hus. They, he said, attacked the morals of the papacy, but he attacked its theology. It is vital to grasp this: Luther's crusade was not ultimately a moral one; it was theological. Of course, the two are intimately related. His attack on indulgences in 1517 was in large part an attack on abusive pastoral practice driven by church greed; but it was also rooted in his changing theology which saw the sale of indulgences as cheapening God's grace, trivialising sin and misleading the laity. He did not attack the practice simply because it was abusive in its practical outworkings but because it rested upon a false view of God and of humanity's status before God.

In the years prior to the protest, Luther had come to see how radically sin affected humanity, that its power was not broken at baptism, that it was so all-consuming that nothing short of death could cure it—and that death he found in the death of

Christ on the cross. Thus, when Tetzel appeared in the neighbouring parish, offering time off purgatory for the payment of a few coppers, Luther was outraged. Here was a man selling God's grace in a way which was not simply financially cheap but was also spiritually cheap. The practice of indulgence sales in the hands of Tetzel had come to bypass the human heart and make salvation something which affected the wallet, not the soul. For Luther this was outrageous in its pastoral implications, because it conned people into a false sense of security; but it was also outrageous theologically, because it reduced the value of Christ's death to a casual financial transaction. Corrupt belief and corrupt practice went hand-in-hand, and the one could not be reformed without the reformation of the other.

This was something which the Catholic Church of the time never seemed to grasp. We must beware of those who always paint the Catholic Church of the sixteenth century in unremittingly dark colours. It was certainly in a state of great theological confusion, and it certainly tolerated a large number of moral abuses; but it also contained many men who wished to see the corruption within its ranks cleared up. There was indeed a Catholic Reformation which sought to purge the Church of the corrupt and dishonest. But there was one fundamental difference between the Catholic Reformation and its counterpart which came to be known as Protestantism: the Catholic Reformation focused on practical, moral abuses; it did not seek to reform the theology of the church. This is why the Protestant Reformation was so important: it sought to address the theological foundations of the church and to reform the whole, root and branch.

God first and foremost

We must be aware that the usefulness of Reformation theology lies in its emphasis upon God. The theologies, the catechisms and the liturgies which flowed from the Reformers' pens all indicate that theirs was a piety which was concerned above all with God. The emphasis of the Reformers was always much more upon the identity and action of God than upon human experience of him. The two are, of course, inextricably linked, but the accent always falls upon the divine half of the equation. This, I suspect, is one of the reasons why Calvin's works give so little insight into the man that he was: he talked little of himself because he was concerned with the proper subject of theology, and that was God.

It is true that Luther was somewhat more expansive on personal themes, but again there is an interesting emphasis in his writings which puts the incarnation, not the action of the Spirit, at the centre. Indeed, his major objection to the Anabaptists and the radicals was their obsessive talk of the Spirit and what the Spirit had taught them or how he had affected them. In contrast, Luther wanted to talk of his own experiences as they related not to some subjective influence of the Spirit on his soul but to God in Christ.

This is in marked contrast to much of what we witness today. I will say more about this in subsequent chapters, but one of the elements which most marks contemporary evangelical piety is the obsession not so much with God as with self. Of course, it is easy to pick on examples from outside one's own immediate tradition. Many of the choruses associated with charismatic evangelicalism, for example, often tell us more about the singer than about the one to whom the song is meant to be addressed in worship. Yet if we simply use the Reformation as a resource for categorising the piety of all other groups as inferior, we will have failed in the basic task of contemporary reformation. There is a great danger in so identifying the way we do things with the way the Reformers did them that we obviate the need for considering true reform of our life and practice. The question we need to ask is whether this God emphasis which we find in the Reformers is as evident in the life of our own churches as we so often assume that it is.

One example would be the practice of giving testimonies in a church service. Now do not misinterpret me here. I do not wish to be seen to be saying that such a practice is intrinsically wrong; but it seems to me to be theologically significant that we often know very little of the detailed religious experiences of the great Reformers. This is not, of course, because they did not have such experiences; it is simply because they seem implicitly to have regarded these experiences as not germane to their public role as church leaders. At the end of the day, the gospel is believed because God—because God—so loved the world that he gave his only begotten Son, and so on. The power and persuasiveness of the gospel lies in the fact that God acted in history to save humanity in and through his Son, Jesus Christ. The experience of this salvation by individual people and by whole churches is a source for rejoicing but should never be allowed to eclipse the emphasis on the great saving acts of God's redemptive history. The gospel is the story of what God has done for sinners in Christ; it is not first and foremost the experience of God by any particular individual; and, if testimonies are to be given in a useful way, they must reflect this fact. Too often, however, testimonies can become nothing more than extended reflections upon individual experiences of God. To make room for this sort of testimony is, I would suggest, to place our own evangelical church life on the path towards liberalism which, at the end of the day, is nothing more than a reduction of religious truth to the religious self-consciousness of the individual or the community.

That is just one example; we can all think of others, such as using the Bible as a book of inspiring thoughts, and Bible studies which never rise beyond the question of what a particular passage means to me or how it has affected my life. The Reformers would certainly not have regarded such a question as irrelevant, but would have set it within the context of first asking what the passage meant for the people of God within the redemptive purposes of God. The answer to the question of personal application would have flowed from the answer to this prior question. The lesson is: let us make sure that God is the emphasis in all of our own life and worship rather than sneering at the lyrics of songs sung in other churches.

The centrality of Christ

The third point I wish to draw from this definition is that it is God in Christ with whom the Reformers have to do. Of all the Reformation insights, this is surely the most vital: that in Christ we see the grace of God towards sinful humanity. Though he considered it not robbery to be equal with God, yet the Son voluntarily condescended to come down and take flesh, to live among all the filth, physical and moral, of this world, that he might bring the sinful, men and women, boys and girls, to heaven, to eternal and wonderful fellowship in glory with the triune God, thus saving them from a lost eternity. It was when Luther came to grasp what God had done in Christ that he truly came to see the seriousness of sin and the radical nature of God's grace in salvation. The same is true for Calvin and the other Reformers: their whole theology hangs together on the person and work of the Lord Jesus Christ, and it is clear that their high view of Christ, their profound understanding of sin and their wonder at the miracle of God's grace are all intimately related. One cannot abandon the one without abandoning the others.

This is a point which often brings out the most indignant self-righteousness within the Reformed evangelical constituency, particularly as we cast our eyes over the charismatic movements of the present time. Look at them, we cry. All they do is talk about their experiences and about the Holy Spirit. Don't they realise that the Holy Spirit witnesses to Christ, and that the true sign of his presence is not that people talk about the Spirit but that they talk about Christ? In doing so, of course, we echo the sentiments of Luther concerning the Anabaptists, to which I have already referred. Now, from a theological perspective, I am in deep sympathy with such an argument and do regard the various streams of the charismatic movement in the United Kingdom today as being defective in various ways, some more seriously so than others. Nevertheless, I worry that the act of comparing ourselves constantly with the charismatics has blinded us to our own lack of Christ-centredness and has bred an unhealthy self-righteousness which not only prevents us implementing true reformation but even blinds us to the fact that true reformation is what we need. Bashing charismatics is simply not the same as having a Christ-centred Christianity, and the two should never be confused.

To be truly Christ-centred, all aspects of our Christian life, from corporate worship to private devotions to the everyday Christian walk, must terminate on Christ. Too often today churches with

a high view of Scripture and of the preaching ministry actually tolerate sermons which, while being
very faithful in a sense to the text, never mention
Christ. Yet if the Reformers' claim that Christ is
the centre of the Bible and that the whole Bible
tells one story, that of God's grace in Christ, then
no sermon worthy of the name Christian can possibly omit speaking of Christ, wherever the chosen
text may be taken from, Old or New Testament.
God-centred sermons must by definition be Christ-
centred sermons if they are to contain even a drop
of grace. Worship songs and prayers should be the
same, focusing not on ourselves or our needs, however important they may be, but on Christ.

This is not to say that our needs have no place in
our prayers or worship songs. There is much in the
Bible that portrays Christ as the response to human
needs: 'Come to me all who are weary, and I will
give you rest'; 'Come to me all who are thirsty and
I will give you drink.' These are certainly needs—to
use the modern jargon, they are 'felt needs'—and
Christ is certainly presenting himself as the answer
to them. But that is the crucial point: Christ himself is identifying the need and offering himself as
the solution. The whole thing is Christ-centred; and
this is something which should feature in our worship emphases.

In short, at stake here is an issue of substantial
emphasis, of what actually lies at the centre. If it is
Christ, well and good; if it is anything else, we need
reformation. Let us remember that a Bible-centred

church is not necessarily the same as a Christ-centred church. There isn't a 'Christian' cult or liberal church in the world, after all, which would not claim to be Bible-centred: it is only as the Bible is understood and applied in terms of its centre, Christ, that the two things, Bible-centredness and Christ-centredness, become one. Let us make sure that our desire to stress the centrality of the Bible is also matched by a desire to stress the centrality of Christ in the Bible.

THE ON-GOING REFORMATION

The Reformation, then, sought to place God in Christ at the centre of its life and thought. We need to appreciate one further thing about this reforming activity, however, and that is that it is essentially a dynamic process rather than a static state of affairs. This is captured neatly in the old Latin motto of Reformed churches across the world: ecclesia reformata semper reformanda est. This translates into English as, 'The reformed church is always in need of reforming.' Now, what does this mean? Surely, once we have placed the Word, both as Christ and as Scripture, at the centre of our life and thought, we are truly reformed and thus in no further need of any more reformation? If only it were that simple! Human beings have an almost infinite capacity for idolatry, and this evidences itself not simply in the current craving for novelty but also in the mindless reaction of refusing to change.

Seeing where the battle lies

The whole point of the Reformation from a theological perspective is that it was more than just a dispute over forms. There are those today who like to speak of different Christian traditions, Roman Catholic, Orthodox, Pentecostal, Evangelical, Reformed, etc. Such talk is conducive in a time when the wider culture as a whole is increasingly pluralist and intolerant of narrow and factional claims to truth. In general, the terminology serves to relativise the differences, reducing them in effect to the level of form. The Roman Catholic and Orthodox Churches have a more sacramental form of worship than, say, the Reformed, who emphasise more the Word written and preached; but the essence of the two, Christ, is fundamentally the same, even despite significant differences in theology. The Reformers, however, would have had no truck with such an approach: as far as they were concerned, the battle was not one between forms or emphases or traditions; it was between those who had the gospel and those who were committed to hiding it or opposing it or abolishing it altogether.

The implication of this is that reform of the church was not, is not, and never will be something which can be achieved by tinkering with outward forms or applying tried and trusted techniques of a kind analogous to the instructions one gets with flat-pack furniture. One thing the church needs to grasp more perhaps than ever before is that its current problems are not the result of failures in technique or form but failures of morality. Now, I need to make it clear exactly what I am and am not saying here.

Failures of morality

First, I am not saying that technique, broadly considered as how the externals of the church operate, is not important. The Reformers were well aware of this: it was one of the basic reasons why they wanted to get rid of the Latin liturgy and the Vulgate Bible. In addition to the defective theology of the former and the inaccuracies of the latter, they were both woefully inadequate for the task which the Reformers wished to see liturgy and Scripture fulfil: intelligible and coherent worship. Let us not forget that, while the Reformation could not have happened without the printing press and without the mass production of books, most people in the sixteenth century were brought in to the Reformation church by word of mouth, by the Word preached in their own language. Thus, vernacular worship forms, both liturgy and Bible translation, were needed if the gospel was to be communicated effectively. This, one could argue, is an issue involving not just theology but also technique. Thus, today there is a need to be sensitive to our cultural context.

But 'sensitive to' does not mean 'capitulate to'— there is a difference and there are aspects of our culture, for example, its sexual mores, to which we cannot accommodate our worship forms without a basic betrayal of the message we have to proclaim. Nevertheless, sanctified common sense dictates that, when we preach to an English congregation, we use the modern vernacular, not that of Chaucer; and so on and so forth. Failure to do so is a failure to live up to the standards set by the Reformers. It may mimic the Reformers in terms of its form, but it fails to come to grips with what the Reformers were actually doing all those years ago.

Second, by claiming that our current crisis represents a failure of morality, I am not saying that the power of the gospel message depends for its efficacy upon the personal morality of the preacher. The Word is the Word; and it is powerful because it is God's Word and accompanied by God's Spirit. The preacher may well be a secret adulterer, but that will not prevent people being converted under his ministry. Indeed, one of the most amazing things about church history is the fact that the kingdom of God progresses so often in the teeth of the immorality and infidelity of the people and their leaders. To declare, then, that the church's current problems are moral is not to forge an unbreakable cause-effect link between our individual behaviour and the effectiveness of the gospel. And thank God that this is so! If such a link existed, who of us here today would ever have been converted? It is only through grace that God enables sinful men and women to lead others to Christ.

31

Third, what I am saying is that we must be aware that the struggle to reform the church should arise out of our willingness to be obedient to God, to seek his face in prayer, and to seek his wisdom in the Scriptures with a view to putting the latter into practice. This, in turn, means that we will constantly be scrutinising our theology and our practice to see where it fails to match up to biblical standards and where therefore it needs to be modified or even abandoned. It is an interesting fact that with neither Luther nor Calvin was the break with the medieval church an instantaneous or immediate thing. In the case of Luther (and probably in the case of Calvin, though we have less biographical detail available), his rejection of church practices such as indulgences and the Mass was based upon his prior understanding and experience of God's grace. It was only in the light of this that he gradually came to realise that contemporary church practice was inadequate and thus needed to be changed through reformation. The Mass, indulgences, the confessional—all of these things ultimately had to go because they failed to do justice to biblical teaching. Luther's was not a reformation which sought to change hearts and minds by changing the structures; rather it was a reformation which changed the structures because of the prior change of heart.

Following biblical principles

This brings us back to that strange saying, ecclesia reformata semper reformanda est, 'the reformed church is always in need of reforming'. The point is simple: reformation is not something which happens at one point in time and then ceases. Indeed, as soon as we rest content with our outward forms—the language used in worship, the Bible translation read from the pulpit, the kind of musical accompaniment, or lack thereof, in the worship service—and rest content with these. More often than not, I suspect, the reasons underlying these debates (on Bible Translations, for example) have more to do with personal preferences with regard to the aesthetics of worship, or a concern that traditions which we have cherished dearly for many years are to be abandoned. Such arguments are simply a reversal of the priorities of true reformation because each is ultimately concerned with the outward practice rather than the belief which underlies the practice. It may be that each of these areas will have a certain form when the Bible is taken to heart and its teachings seriously applied. I myself would want to say that those who take the Bible seriously will not tolerate worship songs with a certain content, will not allow the sermon to be marginalised, and will not countenance certain worship practice. But we need to be constantly examining our practices and procedures by the light of the Word of God in order to make sure that we do what we do because it is biblical and not simply because it is familiar or aesthetically pleasing.

We need only look at the significant differences which emerged among the Reformers themselves on issues such as the Lord's Supper, the correctness of liturgical dress and the relationship of church and state to realise that they themselves were as sinful in their hearts and often as petty in their practices as we are today. Don't forget that Luther regarded all those who rejected the presence of Christ's humanity in the eucharistic elements as being of a different spirit to himself, that is, as basically not being Christian at all—and I suspect that judgement applies to most reading these words. He was a big man and he made big mistakes, along with all his fellow Reformers. Let us not idolise these people but learn from them, for they were simply doing in their day and generation what we seek to do in ours. If the reason for our practices is simply idolatrous approval of the tradition or the status quo, then we must be prepared when the time comes to be honest about this and not to cling to them beyond the length of their usefulness. When we affirm something, it must be for the right reason; and when we reject something it must be for the right reason.

HUMAN SINFULNESS

It is worth remembering here one other aspect of the Reformation's legacy: the clear grasp of human sinfulness which it brought to the fore of theological discussion. For Luther, as for Calvin, the unregenerate heart was corrupted in such a way that it was both impotent, morally and intellectually, for the theological task, and inherently idolatrous. What this meant was that humanity would always seek to make God in its own image, always seek to worship him on its own terms, always seek to worship itself or its own forms than to face up to the experience of standing before God's holiness and coming to him on his own terms. This has, I think, two applications when we think of contemporary reform of our worship.

Our response to the world

First, it limits the importance of listening to the world around us in terms of our practice. Much is made today of what Generation X, the New Age movement, or whatever, is saying to the church. Now, on one level, we certainly want to communicate the gospel in a way that Generation X, New Agers, etc, can understand. As I said above, the Reformers placed communicating the gospel to the laity at the heart of their programme, and we must be aware, for example, that when we preach evangelistically, we do so to a world which no longer has any basic grasp of the Bible's storyline or even of what God is meant to be. I have a colleague at university who teaches Milton's *Paradise Lost* in the English Department and has to preface the course with a lecture on 'Ten Things You Need to Know About God'. This includes such basic elements as the fact that he is perfect and immaterial. This is an indication of how ignorant the western world now is of the Bible.

Having said all this, however, what Generation X and the New Age movement are actually telling the church is that the human heart is ineradicably idolatrous, that men and women will do anything and believe in anything rather than face up to the claims of the triune God on their lives. Thus, let us listen to the world to see what questions it asks, what thoughts it has and what language it uses; but let us set all this within the context of human sinfulness and idolatry and beware of those who conceive of the Reformation of the church in terms which, to put it technically, abolish the distinctions between special and common grace or, in more popular parlance, fail to address the depth of human idolatry.

Our response to ourselves

Second, however, human sinfulness should also make us self-critical. We are redeemed, yet we live between the time of our salvation and our final perfection in heaven. We too are idolatrous. We too, like the children of Israel, are likely to build our sacred cows under the pretext of worshipping the triune God Jehovah. As a result, we need to be constantly examining our own motives for taking the stands which we do on worship and the like. We rightly reject those who wish to see Christianity capitulate to the latest cultural trend, but we need to make sure that in doing so we are not throwing the baby out with the bathwater or simply maintaining tradition because we like it or are comfortable with it.

Our response to the Reformation

This brings me to my last point: we must remember that the Reformation proper happened some five hundred years ago and was, as all historical events are, inextricably bound up with the thought forms and the concerns of its time. This is obviously not to say that it has no relevance for today—the whole thrust of these chapters runs counter to such an assertion. It is, however, to point out that we must remember that we cannot simply leap across the historical ditch and act in the present as men and women did in the past. The writings of the Reformers are not Holy Writ. They were greatly used by God, but they were not inspired in their actions in the way that the figures of redemptive history were. Idolatry, the cult of the saints, and uncritical deference to the authority of tradition are not things from which Protestants are immune.

As I said at the start of this chapter, we must not approach the Reformers as if they could do no wrong; we must rather go to them with an appreciative but critical spirit, appreciative in acknowledging their insights into the Bible's teaching, and critical in remembering that, like us, they were mere sinful mortals capable of disastrous mistakes as well as marvellous achievements. In these chapters, I intend to dwell on the latter rather than the former, but let us remember that only the Scriptures give us true and undefiled knowledge of God; and only faith in Christ, not faith in Luther or Calvin or any mere mortal, can save us.

MEETING THE MAN OF SORROWS

Shortly after the outbreak of the famous indulgence controversy in late 1517 to early 1518, Martin Luther took part in a disputation at Heidelberg where his monastic order, that of the Augustinians, was holding its chapter meeting. It would seem that the Church had, initially at least, considered Luther's protest to be something of a little local difficulty and were inclined to let the Order itself sort the problem out. In retrospect, the decision was a fatal mistake as Luther's protest soon spiralled out of the Church's control; at the time, however, there was little to suggest that the indulgence controversy would have the international repercussions with which we are now all so familiar.

LUTHER'S REFORMATION THEOLOGY

At Heidelberg, Luther presented to the assembled body a series of theses, or propositions for debate.

39

When we read the text of the theses now, it is clear that they must be understood against the background of late medieval theological debates: the meaning of many is obscure to those unfamiliar with the background, and one is almost inclined to wonder why the debate over these theses so impressed those gathered there. The audience, including Martin Bucer, later reformer of Strasbourg who ended his days as Professor of Divinity at Cambridge, were enthralled by what he had to say, although at the time many, including Bucer, missed the theological depth of the argument. The programme which Luther proposed at Heidelberg was little short of revolutionary, espousing a thorough overhaul of theological method in the light of Luther's increasing clarity concerning the nature of true theology. This culminated in a number of theses which have come down to posterity as teaching the 'theology of the cross', an aspect of Lutheran theology which became increasingly obscured in the later Reformation tradition and yet which lies at the heart of Luther's own Reformation theology. Indeed, it is to this that I wish to look now, because it contains, I believe, important truths which the church needs to hear again if it is ever to experience another reformation of its life and teaching.

The nineteenth to twenty-first theses read as follows:

> 19. That person does not deserve to be called a theologian who looks upon

the invisible things of God as though
they were clearly perceptible in those
things which have actually happened
(Rom. 1:20).

20.   He deserves to be called a theologian,
however, who comprehends the visible and manifest things of God seen
through suffering and the cross.

21.   A theologian of glory calls evil good
and good evil. A theologian of the
cross calls the thing what it actually is.

The language used is obscure: 'invisible things';
'theologian of glory'; 'theologian of the cross'. Yet
the thoughts are explosive and reflect the heart of
Luther's Reformation protest.

The theologian of glory

What Luther is rebelling against here is the tendency that he perceived among theologians in his
own day to create a picture of God which reflected
merely humanity's own expectations of what God
should be like. This is what he had in mind when
he referred to the theologian of glory. To take the
most obvious example: most people expect that God
rewards those who do good things. Those who be-
have well and obey God will merit entry into heav-
en. This is because most people assume that God's
justice is very similar to their own.

According to Luther's Reformation theology, however, even the best human works are as filthy rags before God; only the righteousness of Christ can avail to bring about salvation. Thus, my acts of charity, which the theologian calls good on the basis that they are what God wants and will bring me to heaven, are in fact evil. At best, they are morally filthy before God; at worst, they become acts of self righteousness whereby I promote myself and my own efforts as the foundation of my salvation, not the righteousness of Christ. In other words, the theologian of glory, starting with what he or she expects God to be like, has ended up by calling that good (i.e. my own works) which is actually evil.

The theologian of the cross

The theologian of the cross, however, is the one who sees things as they really are, the one who knows what God is really like because his or her thinking about God starts with God's revelation of himself and not with human expectations. Where does this revelation take place for Luther? Primarily in the person of Christ on the cross at Calvary. That is where theology must begin and end; that is the source and the principle by which all theological statements must be judged and understood. This is perhaps Luther's most dramatic and profound insight into the nature of theology, with implications that are little short of shattering.

The cross

The cross itself provides a perfect, indeed, the supreme, example of a place where the theologian of glory and the theologian of the cross would find no common ground. What does the theologian of glory see there? Well, based upon rational, empirical enquiry, one would have to say that the man on the cross is a filthy criminal of some kind. Why else would he be dying such an indescribable death as a punishment? The cross is a disgrace, both by the standards of Roman law and Jewish custom, and thus the one upon whom such a punishment is inflicted must be the lowest kind of criminal imaginable. In addition, one would have to say that he is broken, crushed, defeated. As he dies on the cross, we see no king, no victory over sin, no cause for rejoicing or glorifying the one who hangs there. The eyes of reason, judging on the basis of what we as humans expect, would have to see that the scene as one of darkness, pain and deep personal tragedy. All of these bleak and negative descriptions would seem the only appropriate ways of describing what is taking place if one approaches the cross with human expectations and criteria.

The theologian of the cross, however, approaching the event with the eyes of faith and with the criteria provided by God's revelation of himself, sees a very different picture: not a sinner, but the only sinless man; not defeat, but triumph; not wrath, but mercy. What we have on the cross is not the defeat

43

of a criminal, but the triumph of the king of glory; not the victory of the powers of evil, but the victory of good over evil; not the hopeless curse of God, but the blessing of God by which all may be saved.

The results, then, of coming to the cross with the eyes of faith are theologically dramatic, indeed, revolutionary in the most literal sense of the word: they turn our thoughts about God upside down and demand that all human expectations be brought under the shadow of the cross where their adequacy as human expressions of divine truth can be judged by how God really is and how he really acts towards us. When one wishes to think of God's power and sovereignty, where should one look? Luther's answer would be: to the cross. There, in the brokenness of the suffering Christ the believer sees the triumph and the glory of the God of grace over the world, the flesh and the devil. There, in this strange and powerful contradiction of all our human expectation, is where we see God as he really is towards us, in all his power and glory. Where does one see God's love most dramatically displayed? In the willing submission of Christ to the full weight of divine wrath on the cross. Where does one see God's holiness most clearly? In the terrible agonies of the Son on the cross as he reveals sin's full filthiness and demonstrates how seriously God himself takes it.

LUTHER'S THEOLOGY OF THE CROSS

This, I believe, takes us very close to the heart of Luther's Reformation theology. We are all accustomed to debates about justification by faith, about the authority of Scripture and even about the relationship of the human will to salvation, each of which is a crucial topic. But the theology of the cross, radical and dramatic protest that it was, slipped from the agenda of Protestant theology in a manner which, I believe, impoverished the latter to a not insignificant degree. The Reformation was, after all, a supremely Christ-centred movement in terms of its theological content, and no one theologian expressed this Christ-saturated approach more dramatically than Martin Luther in his theology of the cross. Why this aspect of his thought has come to be so neglected is not immediately obvious—though it has to be said that the theology of the cross never played a particularly central and explicit role in Reformation theology after Luther. But I now want to argue that it is a note which the evangelical church would do well to strike again, particularly if it wishes to draw upon the richness of the Reformation for its contemporary life and practice. The heritage of the Reformation is more than just the doctrine of justification by faith; it is also the theology of the cross; and we do well to listen to Luther on this, as on many other topics.

Suffering

Liberal theology in the twentieth century rediscovered the cross as a central part of the theological enterprise. This was in no small measure due to the reality of suffering, whether in the terrible acts of

45

genocide which littered the century or in the cat-
astrophic poverty endured by many countries. As
suffering became more obviously an integral part
of the human experience, so the liberal theologians
sought to emphasise this aspect of the Bible's teaching, largely, I believe, to justify Christian theology
in the face of such darkness. Like the social gospel
before it, the gospel of suffering grasped something
of the truth within Christianity but emphasised it at
the expense of other fundamental Christian truths,
such as universal personal guilt. Nevertheless, as
evangelicals our task is not to reject something simply because non-evangelicals have taught it, but to
claim the moral high ground by presenting to the
world a theology which is balanced and which reflects the emphases of God's word. Suffering is part
of that, and we should not allow its use by liberals
to distract us from addressing the issue.

The theology of the cross is more than just a way
of looking at God, however. For Luther, it brings
to the fore both the depth of God's love for sinful
humanity, that God himself was willing to undergo
such suffering, weakness and humiliation on behalf
of helpless sinners, and also underlines that suffering
and weakness is a central part of the Christian's
strength experience here on earth. In Christ, God
has so identified himself with humanity as to
become one with fellow humans. He has endured
not only the mundane inconveniences of our
existence but has even suffered in a supreme sense

on our behalf, that suffering which is captured in a deep and inexplicable way in the cry of dereliction on the cross.

These are, of course, deep theological waters, but for Luther the crucial dimension of God's saving power was precisely this profound humiliation of himself in human weakness. He had a saying: Don't give me God without giving me his humanity. The point was simple: it is in the incarnation, in the flesh of Christ, that God both is, and shows himself to be, gracious towards us. Luther rejoiced in the fact that he did not worship a God who was far way, a despot, an abstract and anonymous philosophical principle. No—he worshipped a God who had come close, so close that he even clothed himself in human flesh; a God who was so merciful that he was prepared to welcome sinners into his presence as if they had never sinned; a God who was so loving that he happily freed men and women from all manner of physical and spiritual bondage so that they might know true life; and a God who was so strong that he was prepared to make himself nothing and die that terrible death on the cross in order that human beings should never have to die.

The centrality of Christ's humanity

At the centre of Luther's doctrine of God, then, stands the humanity of Christ, for it is there that God is merciful and gracious. This is why Luther was so concerned to have the humanity present in the eucharist—he could not conceive of God being present in his grace outside of the bounds of his humanity. He overstated the case here, I believe, but the concern to see God's mercy as exclusively revealed in the person of the human Jesus is understandable. Furthermore, not only is it the humanity which stands at the centre for Luther—it is the suffering humanity, for it is on the cross, in the darkness, agony and squalor of that death, that the victorious grace of God is shown forth to the eyes of faith in such a wonderful and mysterious manner. This is why Luther's whole theology can be quite accurately summed up as one protracted attempt to direct men and women to God in human flesh, Jesus of Nazareth, and him as crucified.

A pattern for the church

The theology of the cross does not stop there, however. It is not simply something which has to do with theoretical knowledge of God. The cross is not simply an intellectual puzzle whereby, once we have grasped that all expectations are inverted, we are enabled to decode what is going on and produce our nice, neat and painless theological systems. Life would be a lot easier if that were the case. In fact, the theology of the cross is not simply an example of how God is gracious; it is also the basic pattern for understanding how he is to work in and through us, his church. The theology of the cross is not a cerebral thing; it profoundly affects our Christian experience and existence, making demands upon our whole lives and turning theology into something which controls not just our thoughts, but the very way in which we experience the world around and taste the blessing and fellowship of God himself. Suffering and weakness are not just the way in which Christ triumphs and conquers; they are the way in which we are to triumph and conquer too. In other words, if suffering and weakness are the ways God works in Christ, it is to be expected that these are the ways he will work in those who seek to follow Christ. One does not become a theologian by knowing a lot about God; one becomes a theologian by suffering the torments and feeling the weakness which union with Christ must inevitably bring in its wake.

That message is, of course, one which sits awkwardly with the present age, for a number of reasons. The atrocities of the twentieth century, supremely that of the Holocaust, have raised acute questions about the justice, even the existence, of God. Ever since Job, the problem of why bad things happen to good people has never been very far from the surface, both in rarefied theological and philosophical discussion and in the minds of ordinary men, women and children faced with the horrors of history or personal suffering and bereavement.

In addition to the obvious question of God's justice which these larger issues raise, it must also be acknowledged that one characteristic of the modern consumerism of the West is impatience with any form of inconvenience, not just the serious variety referring to death, illness, etc. One has only to look at the billions of pounds that are made by the cosmetic, pharmaceutical and credit industries to see how little the modern westerner is willing to put up with. Do you have a headache? Pop a painkiller. Are you unhappy with the length of your nose? Get the surgeon to cut it down to the desired size and shape. Do you want that new television set, with all the digital channels, the Nicam sound, etc? Don't bother saving—just put it on the plastic card. Indeed, in a consumer world where self-fulfilment rather than family or social commitments has become the driving force, the question of God's justice in suffering has probably been trivialised to a point unknown in previous history. How many TV chat shows are dominated by concerns about noisy neighbours, rude workmates, disobedient children, unhappy childhoods, unacceptable demands made by families? All are problematic, of course, but they scarcely represent serious suffering or genuine challenges to the existence of the good God as, say, the Holocaust or even the death of a single innocent child.

The theology of the cross, however, acts on the question of suffering in much the same way as it acts upon other theological questions: it inverts human assumptions. The natural question to ask when one is suffering in some way is, 'Why me? Why is this terrible thing happening to me? I've done nothing wrong.' For Luther, the question must be answered by looking to the cross: if suffering, persecution, injustice, hatred and scorn are the lot of Christ, and if it is through these very means that God, in a manner incomprehensible and unexpected, achieves his goal of saving helpless sinners, then are we to expect our lot to be any better? In other words, the question is not so much, 'Why do bad things happen to good people?' as, 'Why do more bad things not happen to good people?'

The point is: the cross is not simply God's saving action on behalf of sinful humanity. Of course, it is never less than that, and that indeed stands at the very heart of its meaning. But it is also a demonstration of how God acts in general, how he achieves those purposes which he intends.

Luther uses a couple of technical terms for this: alien work and proper work. Alien work refers to God's dealing with us in a way we do not expect and which apparently leads to the result we do not desire. The cross is a good example of an alien work: Christ dies, a condemned criminal, and thus what appears to be achieved is simply the defeat of God's purposes. Yet it is God's practice to achieve his proper work, that which he does really intend, through his alien work. So the cross appears to be a defeat but is in fact the means to divine victory. The alien work of death, suffering, wrath and condemnation taking place on the cross is actually the vehicle for achieving life, blessedness, mercy and salvation.

This pattern, of which the cross is the supreme example, is basic for Luther's understanding of the Christian life: God always achieves his proper work in us (i.e. our salvation) through his alien work (our suffering and weakness). To bring us to heaven, he must first, so to speak, cast us into hell; that is, to sample the joys of the freedom of the gospel, we must first be brought to despair of our own righteousness.

In addition, the sacrificial self-giving of God in Christ to humanity provides a pattern for the practical outworking of the Christian life: as Christ gave of himself to the uttermost to serve others, so believers should give of themselves to the uttermost to serve their neighbours.

Finally, as Christ accepted suffering and death as part of his own life and ministry, so those who seek to walk in his footsteps should expect no less. Indeed, for Luther suffering and weakness are the essence of the Christian life, for it is in our suffering and weakness that God achieves his proper work in us: that, as we have noted above, of bringing us to heaven.

PRACTICAL CONSEQUENCES

The implications of this aspect of Reformation teaching are quite simply explosive. For a start, it puts the question of personal suffering and feelings of weakness and inadequacy in perspective. After all, the more Christlike one is, the more prone one must presumably be to suffer and to feel weak and inadequate, for it is in these things that a basic aspect of Christlikeness is to be found. This is not, of course, to say that we are saved by our suffering—far from it. What it means is that, once we are saved, we can expect suffering and weakness as part and parcel of the Christ-centred life. We should, therefore, not be surprised when difficulties arise in our lives for these are an essential part of God's alien work whereby he achieves his proper work within us.

The Christian's expectations

To bring this down to a practical level, Luther's theology of the cross has profound implications for the horizons of expectation within the life of the individual believer and the Christian community as a whole. What is the Christian believer to expect from life? Health, wealth and happiness? Is that how God shows his grace and favour? That is certainly what a theologian of glory would assume: if God is good to me, then he will give me all those things I most want. The values and expectations of a theologian of glory are those of the world around. Thus, spiritual success must be judged in a manner analogous to earthly success, in terms of income, status and general social credibility. But that is not true Christian theology as Luther understands it, for it has no place for the cross. True Christian expectations centre on the cross and involve an acceptance, if not the willing embrace, of the suffering, weakness and marginalisation which inevitably come to those who follow in the footsteps of the Master. These are to be the horizons of expectation of the believer as an individual and of the church as a whole.

Society's expectations

This Reformation insight is, I believe, of critical importance today, for we live in an age when the horizons of expectation within wider society have moved to the point where this kind of theology, the theology of the cross, is totally excluded. Now, I am a good Calvinist and regard all activity that is not gracious activity as fundamentally unChristian, and I regard all thought that is not Christian thought as a form of rebellion against God. Yet I think that expectations from life have shifted very dramatically in the last forty years or so in a direction which has brought us to the point where the theology of the cross is more explicitly opposed to what goes on in society than at any other point in recent history.

The change has been mapped by sociologists who argue that, in the past, individuals conceived of their purpose in life in more social terms. For example, one worked for the good of society as a whole, or one worked to provide a stable home and environment for one's children. The goal of existence was considered to lie outside oneself, in creating a state of affairs which would benefit others. For a variety of reasons, this situation has changed dramatically with respect to the generations which have come to maturity in the sixties and beyond. Then the perspective moved from what one might broadly categorise as social responsibility in all its forms to self-fulfilment. The game of life now is not so much to work for the greater good of society (of which, as one lady once commented, we know that 'there is no such thing') or even of the family but for the happiness of oneself. We put our careers before the welfare of our children, we don't like paying taxes because they take from our purse for the wider society in which we live, we will not put ourselves out for others in any way that might hinder our own career development or leisure time. We must be self-fulfilled before we give ourselves in any way to others.

Opposing values

Immediately one can see how this stands explicitly at odds with any conception we might have of the theology of the cross. In its very essence, Luther's understanding of Christ and of Christianity stands opposed to the gospel of self-fulfilment. Indeed, two more different gospels it would be hard to find, and I think a case could be made, without much exaggeration for arguing that what we see in society now is the most thorough social outworking and application of sin in human history. This is not to say that our times are any more sinful than those which have gone before; it is simply to argue that where sin is concerned, the statement 'what you see is what you get' is perhaps more true than it has ever been.

How this has panned out in wider society is obvious. The vast numbers of medical dramas, of get-rich-quick quizzes and of self-image programmes on TV give a good idea of what obsesses the public: health, wealth and happiness. These three things have become the three golden calves of the contemporary western world because they speak predominantly of personal fulfilment, reinforcing the notion of a human purpose which lies within the self rather than that which lies beyond the self.

In addition, of course, the West has created a religion, that of free market capitalism, which argues that the old social values of family, neighbourhood and responsibility are best served by the rise of unrestricted capitalism. This view is thrust at us from all sides as 'the truth', as if the huge mortgages, credit card bills, Third World debts, etc, generated by such an approach were all benefits for which the world should be grateful. That this is at best a misguided myth, at worst a justification of greed, should require no proof. The more we have, the more we want. The more we earn, the less we want to give away. The more successful within the capitalist framework we are, the more we despise the weak who are crushed by the wheels of commerce. As for family values, one has only to see how tax law has changed in Britain to see that the 'every man and woman for themselves' attitude to production and consumption has eaten away at the family unit for nigh on a generation. Every politician talks up family values and social concern, but none of them will put in place the policies that would reinforce these values because it would cost too much; and

that, of course, is where the rest of us come in—
we won't vote for such policies because that would
mean higher taxes, and, because the needs of others
are greater, that would mean giving up some of our
own potential for self-fulfilment.

I say all this not to make a political point, but to
underline what is happening in the world around.
It is important that we as Christians do not have an
impoverished sense of sin which restricts it to the
areas of not buying Sunday papers or of watching
certain kinds of films. Sin attacks humanity at its
very foundations, at the level of what motivates us
and what ends we strive for; it shapes the very structures of society and of the philosophies which justify those structures; it strives continually to remake
us in its own image; and unless we can see the difference between the kind of values instilled into us
by the world and those which the Bible would have
us develop, we are doomed to be for ever caught in
a web of worldliness that dishonours God.

THE WAY FORWARD FOR THE CHURCH

The purpose of this lecture series is to bring to bear
insights of the Reformers on the church situation of
the present day, and in this case it is, I hope, obvious what I am going to say: one way in which the
church can start to free itself from the framework
of values which it has imbibed from the world is to
reflect long and hard on the theology of the cross.
The cross, after all, was not simply one element

among many in Luther's theological programme: it was its very heart, for it was here that God revealed himself as gracious towards humanity, and it was here that he established what was to be the normative pattern for judging all aspects of Christianity, from theology to the practical nuts and bolts of the Christian life. As such, any programme of reformation which seeks to honour the work of God in and through Luther must take to its heart the message of the cross.

The question at this point, then, is how the church is to take the message of the cross to the heart of its life when it meets as a worshipping community on the Lord's Day and at other times. How is this central Lutheran insight of the suffering and weakness that stands at the heart of the gospel to be translated into our modern world? This is, of course, a difficult question, but I want to offer one or two pointers for reflection as to what this might entail.

Showing the relevance of the cross

The first thing to point out is that suffering and weakness, while we do our best in our consumerist society to eliminate them, alleviate them or hide them away, are still very much with us. As a university lecturer, every year I have come across students who should, in theory, be happy with their lot—successful, attractive, bright—and yet who suffer from terrible inner torments, whether caused by loneliness, work or financial pressures, family

expectations or whatever. Even among the successful middle classes of England, Wales, or Scotland,
therefore, feelings of pain, emptiness and weakness
are still an ever present reality for many. To this one
can add the amount of physical and mental illness
there is in our nation, the poverty, the horrendous
levels of physical and sexual abuse, the number of
marriages and families which end up on the scrap
heap year by year.

We may belong to a society that exalts health,
wealth, happiness and self-fulfilment, but even its
strongest advocates must concede that the results are
far from uniformly successful; and, if the National
Lottery, with its illusory promise of quick wealth,
has come to function in our godless world rather as
Marx thought religion did in the Industrial Revolution—as opium, as a means of dulling the pain and
drudgery of everyday life—it could not do so unless
everyday life was, for most, an often painful drudge.

As a result, the message of the cross regarding
the God who reveals himself and his grace in and
through the suffering and weakness of his Son is
surely one which is most appropriate for the present
day as both an evangelistic and pastoral tool. On the
one hand, it stands in flat contradiction and utter
condemnation of any gospel of self-fulfilment that
might be peddled as if it were the real truth; on the
other hand, it points people towards the God who is
not at all far off but who has, on the contrary, entered
into the very depths of human existence, even to
taking human flesh and undergoing the torment

and the isolation of the cross. We do not have a God who lives in a far country, after all, but a God who has come as close to us and to our experiences as it is possible to come. Are you suffering? Then Jesus Christ has suffered too and knows in a deep and mysterious way what you are going through. Are you lonely and isolated? Then Jesus Christ has been lonely and isolated too. The brokenness of the created order engendered by sin is laid bare in the life and work of Christ. We need to show in our preaching and teaching that God himself is fully aware of the darkness that now engulfs his creation and has not abandoned the world but entered the world in order to work salvation. Our God is not the distant God of the Deists but one who knows precisely how damaged the world as a whole, and we as individuals, have been by sin.

This is not to reduce Christ to one who simply meets the human needs which are exacerbated by the urbanised, consumer culture in which we live. Such a 'gospel as therapy' approach would itself be little more than a religious spin on the underlying concerns of our secular culture, a kind of 'theology as psychology'. It is rather to indicate at the outset that suffering and weakness, in whatever form they may come, are an inevitable part of life in a sinful, broken world and are therefore something with which the church must genuinely grapple if it is to take seriously the God of the cross. There are plenty of people in the church who argue that it should be more 'user friendly' and more open to those outside; and so it must. But if by that is meant, as is so often the case, that the church must compete with secular entertainment in order to 'pull in the punters' by constantly thrilling its congregations and alleviating their boredom, then that is wrong. That is simply a replication of the world's approach to suffering which is all too often little more than an attempt to eliminate it by burying it under trivia. It is, as Luther might have put it, an application of the theology of glory to a situation which demands a theology of the cross. I confess that such 'gospel as entertainment' approaches sicken me to my very core and are little short of a blasphemous trivialisation of the cross of Calvary.

We are not in the business of clowning around to make ourselves relevant through entertainment. The church first makes itself relevant by facing up to life as it really is, life as the Bible demonstrates it really is, and not by offering yet more amusing diversions to dull the pain of a mortality made tedious by an excess of possessions and a dearth of real, human relationships. And the church faces up to reality by facing up to God's Word and to the man who stands at the centre of the Bible and was himself the Word incarnate, the suffering Christ on the cross. We are to point people to him as the answer to their suffering because only in the context of Christ will the suffering and brokenness of this world of sin and selfishness come to make some kind of sense and find its resolution. Obviously, to an extent, evil and its consequences will always remain a profound and ugly mystery; but knowing that human sin has been overcome by Christ who himself suffered and died on the cross will at least serve to put the problem in perspective and give us realistic expectations of what this world has to offer to the one who seeks to follow in the footsteps of the Master.

My first point, then, is that suffering, and all the language and theology that goes with it, is not something which today's double income, designer label families may want to talk about, but it is something which, in one form or another, is inevitably familiar. How could it be otherwise, an evangelical might ask, when the world's relationship to God is so damaged and disrupted by sin? Let us not therefore blunt the message of the cross out of some misguided belief that in so doing we are making ourselves relevant.

Living out the full meaning of the cross
The second point, following on from the first, is that this should lead to a deeper appropriation of the cross than is often the case in evangelical circles. Now at this point I want to make it quite clear that I stand foursquare with those who make penal substitution the central model for understanding the cross and the central message to be preached when the issue of the cross is addressed. That this doctrine is so widely rejected seems to me totally bizarre as few doctrines are so clearly taught in Scripture as this one. All that I shall go on to say must be read against that background, lest any think

that I am joining the slowly lengthening line of evangelical theologians who have downgraded and even abandoned the notion over recent decades. Nevertheless, it sometimes seems that, perhaps in reaction to this trend, evangelical preaching of the cross is expressed almost exclusively in this category, with Christ's incarnation and humanity functioning as little more than an instrument whereby the act of penal substitution became possible. This, I would argue, impoverishes our understanding of the cross and robs congregations of other aspects of Christ's incarnate work, particularly on the cross, from which great spiritual benefit might be reaped.

First, a cross-centred church understands the true theological status of weakness. The church was born in weakness, born from the death of one who was weak, despised and hated, who by all outward, earthly standards was an abject failure at the moment of his death. In addition, during his life the Christ of the Gospels was profoundly concerned with the lives of those members of society who were broken, weak, dispossessed. We see him ministering to the woman who had been crippled by a lifetime of bleeding, to the poor demoniac whose life was in tatters, and, perhaps most moving of all, weeping outside the tomb of his friend when confronted with the outrage that is death. Imagine that the one who did this could have remained in heaven, dwelling in eternal, blissful communion with his Father. See the power of God's grace that shines through his willingness to become so weak. Was there ever such strength in such weakness? Did the world ever see such a marvellous reversal of status, such an inversion of the expected? Can we ever come to grasp what gracious and miraculous condescension lies in those words 'and the Word became flesh'? Such weakness; such strength! Let us therefore meditate more upon the miracle that is the incarnation, for what it tells us about God's grace towards fallen humanity.

In the light of this, of course, one of the most disturbing things about the church in Britain today has to be its almost exclusively middle class make up. For all that non Christians often talk about Christianity as a crutch, those who attend church on a Sunday are, by and large, not the weak members of society but those who earn good salaries, have pleasant families, enjoy a certain influence and status within their chosen sphere and who, outwardly at least, have no obvious need of a crutch, spiritual or otherwise, to get them through life. Where in our churches are all the poor and the weak, those whom the Bible seems to indicate we should expect to see there? Why are our churches not making any significant impact upon those for whom pain and suffering are such daily realities, unrelieved by the various anaesthetics which the consumer society offers? Is it not a rebuke to us that the church is growing fastest in those parts of the world where suffering is part and parcel of life? I suspect that we need to think very carefully about our church life in relation to the cross. Christ came for the weak, those who were marginalised, despairing and despised. Is this a significant factor in our own church life? If not, why not? Could it be because of our failure to allow our agenda to be set by the priorities of Christ?

In addition, let our churches be places where those who have made themselves weak for Christ's sake can find support and comfort. Churches are full of a variety of weak people, be they parents who have given up an extra income to provide their pre-school children with a Christian home environment or those who have chosen a life of celibacy in order to fight same-sex temptations or those who wrestle with all manner of other temptations. Yet our pulpits are often silent on these issues, quietly projecting an image of Christianity as one long street party. But those who choose the difficult path of obedience in any walk of life, be it in terms of work or sexuality or whatever, need to be supported pastorally, need to be reminded that their sacrifice is worthwhile, that the weakness they feel and experience as part of a principled stand is both inevitable and will reap God's ultimate blessing, if not in the way we might humanly expect. We should not presume that congregations are full of the strong and the self-sufficient, whatever their outward appearance might lead us to believe. We need to be constantly alert, constantly encouraging, lest those who feel weak collapse under the strain of having to appear successful and strong all of the time. By putting weakness at the centre of the church's pastoral agenda, we can minister more effectively and more biblically to many of those in church on a Sunday.

Second, let us beware of allowing our churches to be hijacked by those who propose technique as the solution to our problems. This is particularly relevant at the present time, when the managerial mentality, based as it is upon the twin foundations of control and efficiency, is creeping into all aspects of our lives. Control and efficiency are, of course, not bad in themselves and can be highly beneficial, but the church was born out of weakness, the weakness of the cross. Therein lay its strength, for therein lay its contradiction of worldly power and of human expectation. Should we therefore be overly concerned with efficiency, power and influence? Christ himself triumphed by doing what any management guru would regard as completely nonsensical: he threw away the chance of conventional power and influence and went up to Jerusalem knowing that there he would be seized and executed. By modern standards, this was idiotic behaviour. He should have used the powers of earthly influence the devil offered to him; he should have won the authorities over to his way of thinking by selling it to them in a way they would understand; and he should not have exposed himself to persecution until such time as his power-base or public image was secure. Thankfully, Christ's way is not ours; and salvation was the result.

Weakness was also the hallmark of Paul's ministry. Look at what he says in the letters to the Corinthians:

he was not physically impressive; he did not come to them as a slick public speaker; he came in weakness not in strength. Not exactly a model of contemporary spin-doctoring or PR, was he? Not a particularly attractive figure to those outside. Not the kind of guy whose picture you would put on the cover of an evangelistic magazine. But therein lay the power of his ministry—his very weakness brought more glory to God as his ministry produced its fruit.

Thus, when we plan our church life and judge its success, let us not be guided by management technique or modern theories of presentation and influence. The basic principles of church life and practice are laid down in the Bible and are exemplified in the lives of biblical saints. Is the church weak and despised by society at the moment? Well, that is sad; but on another level, who cares? We are not meant to be respectable, to have political influence, to be an organisation that those outside admire for our slickness and savvy. We are meant to be those who preach Christ to the world around us both in our words and our deeds. I find it worrying when evangelical success comes to be measured in the categories of worldly success for precisely this reason: we are not meant to be successful by worldly standards; we are meant to be faithful by biblical standards; and the example of Christ indicates that these two things are, at the end of the day, implacably opposed to each other.

Third, let us place a realistic view of suffering and weakness back on the agenda of the church in its preaching, its singing, indeed, in all aspects of its worship. Let us recapture again the emphases of, for example, the Psalms, embodying as they do a realistic attitude both to rejoicing and to lamentation. Only then can we offer biblical support to those who are suffering agonies in their own lives. I have become increasingly concerned over recent years by what I call the 'macho' evangelical culture within which we live, where doubt, darkness and sorrow are excluded from our horizons of expectation. We are constantly told in sermons about the present delights of the Christian life; our songs speak of nothing but the triumphs of the Christian spirit; and Christian joy is equated too often with a state of emotional happiness and contentment. In other words, Christianity is presented as the answer to the immediate demands of the consumer culture. This is simply not true and is spiritually and pastorally disastrous. Technically speaking, it involves an over-realised eschatology; in layman's terms, it is totally unrealistic and unbiblical, expecting heaven on earth in the here and now. Until we can get rid of the surreptitious influence of comfort-seeking consumerism on our lives and worship, we are unlikely to understand what it is exactly that the cross tells us about the nature of Christianity and of God himself.

Luther, of course, while he lived a life which involved much personal danger and not a little discomfort, died peacefully in his bed. That was not the case with many of those since then who have been inspired by his teaching. Like those in Hebrews 11, many early Protestants and many since gave up home, family, comfort and ultimately lives for the gospel of the one who suffered and died on the cross for us men and women and our salvation. Let us take time every day to remind ourselves that we follow a king, but a king whose crown came through making himself of no account and dying a terrible death on the cross. There is a lesson there which no words from me and no amount of meditation by you can ever fully grasp.

3 THE ORACLES OF GOD

When one surveys the mass of books printed, sermons preached, commentaries and pamphlets written during the Reformation, it is quite clear that it was a movement of words—written words, printed words, spoken words. Indeed, occurring at a point in history when the printing industry was just getting into its stride, it could hardly have been anything else. The Reformation simply could not have happened at any other point in previous history for precisely this reason: its dependence upon the new technology for disseminating its programme. And yet the movement was ultimately not simply a movement of words—that would have made it scarcely more than part of a wider cultural, educational and technological revolution; no, it was above all a movement of the Word—incarnate in Christ and written down in the Scriptures.

THE WORD AND THE REFORMATION

Where, Luther asked, can I find a gracious God? In Christ, in the Word, written and preached, was the answer—and, given the high levels of illiteracy at the time, we must not allow the importance of the printing press to obscure the fact that most sixteenth-century converts to Reformation Christianity heard about the gospel by word of mouth, not the printed page, a crucial point to make to those postmodern popularisers who see the Reformation as too bookish.

This insight of Luther concerning the Word and the words was shared by all the other major Reformers. Indeed, in the Reformed tradition itself even church architecture, with its location of the pulpit not the altar as the focal point, reflected this emphasis upon Bible and sermon. The displacement of the altar represented more graphically than anything else the movement away from a worship based on the sacraments to a worship based upon the word; and this was underlined by the Reformers' insistence that there could be no sacrament without the word, for sacraments were a sign of promise, and thus they needed to be performed within the context of the promise being proclaimed by word of mouth.

The reality then, the challenge today

It is here, then, that we come at last to the very heart of Reformation theology in terms of its practical foundation; for it is here that we come to that which was the normative source of belief and practice for the Reformers; and here also, dare I say it is where we come to the most difficult and perhaps most controversial part of the Reformation legacy today. For the Reformation emphasis upon the Word written and preached represents a profound challenge to the church of today as it seeks to proclaim the gospel to the contemporary world. The reason, of course, is that we now live in a society where the written word and the spoken word are no longer as central to the wider culture as perhaps they once were.

How often are we told that people will not come to an evangelistic service in which the main event is a sermon because people are no longer as willing as perhaps they might once have been to sit and listen to one man speaking? How frequently does it emerge that not even Christians read their Bibles regularly, and that in part because the reading of printed material has been relegated in the popular sphere almost exclusively to airport novels and tabloid newspapers? The whole of our culture is moving away from being centred on the printed page to other media of communication, above all that ubiquitous box of almost total trivia which sits in the corner of our lounges. Given the impact of this even within the Christian church, the question becomes one of how we can continue to be faithful to the Bible-centred emphases of the Reformers while yet speaking boldly to our day and generation.

THE BIBLE: GOD'S WORD

The first thing we need to do is to remind ourselves of what the Bible actually is. It was only because Luther and his fellow Reformers believed that the Bible was God's Word, and was the only way in which they could come to know of God's grace in Christ, that it took on its central role in their lives and their churches. For the Reformers, the Bible was not just a repository of truth; it was the very channel by which God still savingly spoke to his people. The first paragraph of the first article of the Second Helvetic Confession of 1566 puts it thus:

> We believe and confess that the canonical Scriptures of the Prophets and the Apostles of each Testament are the very true word of God and have sufficient authority from themselves, not from men. For God himself spoke to the Patriarchs, the Prophets, and the Apostles, and still speaks to us through the holy Scriptures.

Inspired in its origin

The Scriptures, then, were for the Reformers the means by which God spoke to them. This had two basic dimensions. One was the idea that the Scriptures were themselves inspired, given, if you like, by God to the church as a revelation of himself. We must be careful here. This does not mean that all the Scriptures do the same thing. There are in the Bible a variety of types of literature: histories, songs of praise, cries of lamentation, statements of

74

theological truth about God. When the Reformers held to the full inspiration of all the Scriptures, they did not reduce all of Scripture to the level of information; Scripture contains a number of literary genres and forms and so does various different things. Nor did they reduce all of Scripture to the same level of importance. Clearly, the promise to Abraham and the coming of the Messiah are of more direct importance to the central story of salvation than some of the details of, say, the battle narratives. This is not to say that all scriptural statements are not true in the way God intended them; they most certainly are; but it is simply to point out that some are of more earth-shattering significance than others. In a very deep sense, however, Scripture does not just contain God's word, it is God's Word. This does not mean that it replaces Christ any more than a love letter replaces my wife. It serves rather in the interim as our means of knowing him and of knowing his will. In heaven, we will not need the Bible, for we shall see him face to face—and that is an important point to make over against those who accuse evangelicals of replacing a relationship with a person with a relationship with a book. We emphatically do not; we have a personal relationship with Christ here and now but only through the book.

Inspired in its reception

The Bible, then, is inspired in that it is breathed out by God, and is true in all of its statements in the sense that God himself intended them to be true. But this is only half the story. The Reformers were also very strong on the present inspiration of the Word, that the Word, when read or preached correctly, came with great power because of the intimate relationship which it enjoys with the Spirit of God. When the Word is read, when the Word is preached, the Spirit is so entwined with the Word that it is supremely powerful with a power that derives from this immediate inspiration. William Tyndale expresses it in dramatic fashion:

> When the evangelion is preached, the Spirit of God entereth into them which God hath ordained and appointed unto eternal life, and openeth their inward eyes, and worketh belief in them. When the woeful consciences taste how sweet a thing the bitter death of Christ is, how merciful and loving God is through Christ's purchasing and merits, they begin to love again and to consent to the law of God, how that it is good, and ought to be so, and that God is righteous which made it. (Taken from the preface to the 1525 New Testament)

Here is the power of the Word: that it is the channel or the instrument by which the Spirit is able to work his awesome act of turning round a human being. That is the power of inspiration here and now, indicating that, in dealing with Scripture, we are dealing with a most potent spiritual force.

Misunderstanding the purpose of the Bible

Given this, it seems to me that much of the popular attitude among Christians towards the Bible really reflects a basic failure to understand exactly what it is with which we are dealing. We are all, I guess, familiar with the kinds of Christians who will declare that they have not only the Bible but also the Holy Spirit as a source of guidance and knowledge of God. Such people have failed to understand the role which the Bible itself allots to the Holy Spirit: that of witness to Christ in and through the Scriptures. They have also failed to appreciate that the Bible is, in a very important sense, sufficient for the task for which it is intended, and that there is no revelation independent of or beyond that relating to the redemptive history which culminates in Christ. This is not to say that we are not each guided by the Lord in our daily Christian lives; but it is to say that such guidance will inevitably centre on and be in conformity with the larger teaching of the Bible. Were these things understood, then the kind of opposition between Bible and Spirit which seems so often to underlie such declarations would simply disappear.

Misusing the Bible

There is, however, an equally inadequate tendency within evangelical circles to pay lip service to the Bible as an inspired book while using it in practice as merely an inspiring book. This is most obvious in the common tendency to use the Bible as a collection of blessed thoughts, as a series of quaint literary pegs upon which to hang personal experiences, or as a sort of almanac out of which God is able to speak in some intangible and mystical way. There is a sense in which this view underlies the kinds of meetings where individuals are asked to tell of a particular passage which has spoken to them powerfully over recent months. Sometimes they will bring up a passage and demonstrate a clear understanding of its meaning in terms of redemptive history and personal salvation; at other times, they seem to be using the Bible as their non-Christian friends might use a horoscope: a pious platitude which just happens to give some comfort or confirm some other thought they have had. This idea also lies behind those types of Bible studies at which many of us have been present when everybody's view of what a passage means is allowed to carry equal weight, as if that was what the Reformers intended when they placed the Bible in the hands of everyone and argued for the essential perspicuity of Scripture. The response which Scripture elicits in the reader is, of course, of vital importance; but the response itself should be shaped by the Bible text properly understood, not bent to suit our own situation; and it only elicits that response because it is true; it is inspiring because it is first of all inspired. Thus, the inspiration of the Bible is to be the underlying factor which shapes our response to it.

Such abuses are in part the result of the church context in which people develop as Christians and in which they learn how to read and to use the Bible. Preaching and worship which seldom rises above the level of immediate experience or practical application, which has an almost entirely pragmatic focus, is a breeding ground for precisely this kind of thing. In such a context, the Bible functions not so much as an inspired book, saying and doing what God wants it to say and do, but an inspirational book, saying and doing what we, perhaps unconsciously, want it to say and do to us.

IN WHAT WAY IS THE BIBLE UNIQUE?

Now the Reformers regarded the Bible first and foremost as God's Word to humanity, inspired by the Holy Spirit and applied to the church and to the individual by the Holy Spirit. These are truths which are no doubt regularly hammered home in most Reformed evangelical services.

Confusion

Yet, at a grass-roots level, even within Reformed evangelical churches the same mistakes continue to be made. Just teaching the doctrine in a straight manner does not seem to have the desired effect. Yes, we hear from pulpits that the Bible is true, and indeed it would seem today that within many evangelical churches, at least at the grass-roots level, the idea that the Bible is true and trustworthy is not seriously questioned by many people. Ask the believer next to you in the pew whether the Scriptures are true, and you will invariably get an affirmative answer. Yet ask how this differs from the truth of your car manual, or what difference it should make to the way the Bible is used and read, and you may well find the answers somewhat less confident and sure-footed.

That the Bible is true is accepted; what is not clearly understood is what the implications of this truth and trustworthiness are. After all, whatever the intellectual commitment to inspiration, if the Bible is in practice treated as special simply because it is inspiring, it is not obvious why the Bible should not share its special place in the church with other 'inspiring' pieces of literature, from Spurgeon's *Morning and Evening* to Shakespeare and beyond. If I can find comfort in the soliloquies in *Hamlet*, why should this not feature in my church fellowship discussions as well?

The need for clear teaching
The Bible's uniqueness, not simply as human reflection upon the revelation of God but as part and parcel of the revelation of God, needs to be brought home to the congregation. This is where the role of the minister is so important. He must not simply declare the Bible to be true but demonstrate in his teaching and preaching what it means to say that the Bible is true and what the significance of this fact is. After all, my car maintenance manual

is true and accurate; my bus timetable is true and accurate; the TV listings in my magazine are true and accurate. Simply declaring that the Bible is true and accurate is not sufficient in and of itself to tell me why the Bible is especially significant or how it should be used. It is only when the content of the Bible is presented within a framework which applies its truth, that progress is actually made in my understanding of the Bible.

This is one of the reasons, I believe, why the Reformers spent comparatively little time reflecting on whether the Bible was true or not. Obviously, the critical challenges were not as great as they would become in subsequent years, so there was less need to emphasise this point; but also, in the minds of the Reformers, the doctrines of inspiration and authority were inseparable from issues relating to the purpose of Scripture as God's Word. The Bible was not simply the truth; it was the truth about God; and it was this which made it unique and authoritative.

What is needed above all at the present time, then, is a ministry which handles the Word of God with respect and which impresses on the congregation not just the fact that God's Word is true and powerful, but why it is so and what the significance of this is. The only way that one can consistently do this, I believe, is through systematic expository preaching, which impresses upon congregations the fact that the Bible ultimately tells one story, that of humanity's fall and redemption, and contains one history, that of God's dealings with men and women, culminating in the person and work of the Lord Jesus Christ.

The Bible is not, important, after all, because it warms my heart or inspires more than, say, a love letter from my wife. Indeed, such a letter would no doubt often have much greater emotional impact on me than many passages of the Bible. No, it is the fact that the Bible centres on Christ, witnessed to by the Holy Spirit both in the act of inspiring its composition and applying it to my heart, which makes it unique in a way that my wife's love letter, while special to me, can never be.

THE PULPIT

The first place, then, in which church reformation starts is the pulpit. At this point we do need to grasp that the emphasis in the Reformation both on the Word written and the Word preached was not simply a theologically neutral move. Yes, the Reformation occurs at a point in history when western culture in general was shifting away from the aesthetic and the visual towards the literary and verbal; but this happy circumstance should not lead us to relativise this aspect of the Reformers' programme. The Word written and the Word preached are both central to Christianity and are not simply cultural forms which can be shed when culture moves on.

The sermon: its importance

Preaching in particular was an essential part of the theological message and worship of the Reformers: with a theology that focused upon issues such as law, covenant and promise, stressing that at the centre stood a God who was essentially personal, the verbal dimension of the Reformers' theology was of the very essence of what they were doing. After all, a promise involves a statement with words; a command involves a statement with words; the very nature of personhood demands that we have the ability to express ourselves to others and that, with very, very few exceptions, generally involves some kind of verbal expression at some point. We simply cannot abandon this verbal dimension of Reformation theology without changing that theology itself into something which is basically different. For example, a sacramental theology, where sacraments are performed without a wider verbal reference to promise, may have an aesthetic appeal to postmodern people, but that does not stop it from being simply a dumb mysticism and nothing to do with either the God of the Bible or the theology of the Reformers.

Whatever experts on communication might like to tell us about the best ways of communicating with modern/postmodern people, we would do well to bear in mind James Packer's point that preaching is not simply communication; it is far more than that, in that it actually brings Christ, God himself, to the congregation. The sermon may be made up of words, but what takes place is far more than the mere transmission of information; the Holy Spirit uses those words to point to Christ, to create faith in Christ, and thus to unite individuals to Christ. It is only as Word and Spirit work together that people are confronted with the claims of Christ in a way that truly challenges and changes them.

The gospel is the power of God unto salvation. It is no mere advertising pitch—which is what, it seems to me, so many of the postmodern evangelical gurus think it is. Indeed, it has become almost commonplace to argue that the reason individuals do not become Christians is because the message is being communicated in the wrong way. Thus, the problem is made to appear less the rebellious human heart and more the inadequacy of the communication method. Such an attitude speaks volumes about the way in which the underlying philosophies of consumerism and western capitalism have infiltrated the theology of the evangelical church and found fertile ground in a theological climate which has largely repudiated the biblical, Pauline and Augustinian understanding of God's grace and human nature for an insipid Pelagianism and a superficial understanding of Christian conversion.

The sermon: its limitations
Having said that, I confess that I do find myself in agreement with the postmodern evangelical gurus

on one issue: sermons certainly are inadequate for the task of bringing men and women to Christ. No Reformer ever preached the gospel simply because he thought this method was the best way of selling Christianity. And many of the accounts of services indicate that congregations had no more patience with sermons then than they do now, the only difference being that then they had to be present, and now they have the option of doing something more entertaining.

Where I differ from these gurus is in my analysis of the human condition and the nature of salvation. If we were to agree with them in seeing human beings as always searching for God, as having an innate spirituality which leads them to yearn for deeper and more authentic spiritual experiences, then we could regard the current interest in alternative religions as a positive sign and see our own task as presenting to the spiritual consumer our own product, Christianity, as a more adequate means of fulfilling the so-called 'felt needs' of individuals. If, however, in line with biblical, historic Christianity, supremely that of the Reformers, we regard human beings as sinful and turned inwards towards self, then we see the hunger for alternative religions not as a sign of spiritual yearning but as yet one more example of humanity's infinite capacity to turn even its own innate knowledge that there is something higher than itself into an act of sheer moral and theological rebellion. Make no mistake; much of the trendy

85

stuff coming from the postmodern evangelicals is built on a profoundly optimistic and thus deeply flawed understanding of human nature; and their proposed evangelistic methodologies are shaped by this flawed understanding.

The sermon: God's method

For those, however, standing in the line of the Reformers, humanity, even in its highest natural spiritual exercises, is in a state of utter rebellion against God, and no elaborate string of words, no compelling argument, no passionate speech will ever bring a single individual to Christ. It is only as those words bring with them the Holy Spirit of God bearing witness to Christ that the sermon becomes adequate to its task. Thus, we preach, we speak the words of God not because this is the marketing method most likely to appeal to the unbeliever but simply because this is God's appointed means of coming to individuals and bringing them to faith. Indeed, precisely because it is so weak and hopeless by the world's standards, it brings that much more glory to God when souls are saved and lives turned round through this medium.

Of course we must use language with which the congregation is familiar; of course we must be aware that we are talking to people in the twenty-first century and not the sixteenth; and of course we must be culturally sensitive in what we say; but preach we must because this is God's chosen means of spreading the news of the kingdom. Preaching is not just a communication technique, and must never be considered as such; it is bringing the very words of God to bear upon the life and needs of sinners and of the congregations of God's people. For this reason, if for no other, the sermon must remain central in our worship.

When preaching fails

Furthermore, it is surely no coincidence that the marginalising of the sermon in evangelical life has led not so much to a collapse in zeal for the gospel—for there are many, particularly young people, who come from churches where preaching is not central yet have an enviable zeal—but it has led to a dramatic decline among the laity in knowledge of exactly what that gospel is. Working with evangelical students, it never ceases to astound me how little some of them know. Yes, they love Christ and trust him for forgiveness; but ask them why they have confidence that he forgives them or what the cross achieved, and one is often confronted with a reply which speaks about some nebulous experience or feeling which they have rather than a reference to the cross or to covenant promises.

The reason for this lack is almost always their church background: fellowships where great emphasis may well be placed upon a vital and vibrant Christian life but where preaching is at a discount. The result is that their minds are empty of great

Christian truths and their faith has less than fully stable foundations, being built on pious experiences rather than a well-thought-out biblical and doctrinal worldview rooted in the identity of God himself as found in his revelation. We need to know that we can be confident that God is faithful because of what he has done throughout history, not because we ourselves had some experience at some point in time; and how are we to know this unless somebody tells us?

The preacher's responsibility

The first thing that a preacher needs to realise, therefore, is the seriousness of the task he is undertaking: on his shoulders rests the responsibility of giving his people solid rock on which to build their lives; and in preaching, he is moving the divine Word of God from the divinely inspired text through the words of his sermon to the hearts and minds of his people. He is thus handling, so to speak, the Word of God, something which is both an immense privilege and an awesome responsibility. He must therefore take care that he gets it right and that his attitude towards the task is one appropriate to its gravity. As Richard Baxter declared, 'I preached as a dying man to dying men.' The pulpit was thus no place for clowning or levity or entertaining his congregation; every Sunday it was a place where, perhaps for the last time, he had an opportunity of speaking to men and women about the great things of God. We, of course, live in age where entertainment is one of the be-all-and-end-alls of life; but Christianity is always to an extent counter-cultural, and this is one point on which we cannot afford to be anything else.

The preaching ministry is thus something which should not be entered into lightly; nor is the sermon something which either minister or congregation should approach in a light or trivial manner. The preacher has the responsibility of both expounding God's truth and of doing so in a manner which confronts his congregation with the awesomeness of God's greatness and holiness and the vastness of his grace and love. It takes, therefore, a particular kind of man with a particular calling to perform this task.

THE PREACHER'S TRAINING

The Reformation emphasis on the Word does not just lead to an emphasis on the seriousness of the minster's calling and the task he is to perform; it should also shape the vision for the kind of education and training he is to receive before entering the pulpit. The minister is to be a man who possesses various skills in addition to his love for the gospel and his love for his fellow men and women, Christian and non-Christian. A church which is continually reforming itself in accordance with the Word of God is going to be a church where its leaders are men who understand the Word of God. Now, ministerial training is a vast subject and I could not tackle all the issues, even if I were competent so to do; but there are a number of factors which Reformation theology brought to the fore. I give them in no particular order of priority.

Language study

First, the minister should have some grasp of biblical languages. This is not essential—there have been some notable ministries where the preacher has had little or no linguistic competence. Nevertheless, it is the Hebrew, Aramaic and Greek texts which were inspired, not the King James' or any other version. When the Reformers placed the inspired Word at the centre of their reforming programme, they also provided the dynamic for the growth of linguistic studies precisely because the original texts were so important to the Protestant principle of Scripture alone. Now, studying the biblical languages is almost the monopoly of conservative theological colleges for the same basic reason: a high view of inspiration demands that church leaders get to grips with the original biblical text. This is not to argue for the parading of learning in the pulpit. Education should never be used as a basis for separating minister from people and thus the creation of a new priesthood. Indeed, Calvin himself never referred to the Hebrew or the Greek in his sermons. No, the only reason for acquiring such skills is so that the minister can get closer to the original text, and thus closer to the very mind of God Himself, than any translation will ever permit, however excellent such may be.

Salvation history

Second, the minister should have a sound grasp of the overall theological and historical shape of the Bible. The Bible tells one story, albeit through narratives offering different perspectives; it contains one theology, albeit through books with diverse theological perspectives; and it is therefore to be read, understood and preached as one whole. Atomistic exegesis of isolated texts, thematic preaching on the minister's hobby-horse of the month, and any sermon which fails to set the teaching of any given passage within the sweep of redemptive history as a whole is simply not up to scratch. There is a need therefore not just for the teaching of biblical languages but for the teaching of biblical theology proper, a theology which respects the Bible's historical structure as being part of its very theological structure and thus enables the preacher to move from text to sermon in an appropriate manner.

It is worth noting at this point that what I say here about the minister applies in much the same way to the Sunday School teacher. In Sunday School, the teacher is charged not simply with giving children the basic Bible stories but also with instilling into them the basic tools they need for connecting all the different bits of the Bible together. Graham Goldsworthy from Moore Theological College has gone as far as to say that no one should be allowed to teach Sunday School without a basic grounding in biblical theology. Perhaps that goes a little too far, but certainly all teachers should aspire to fitting the grand narrative of the Bible together in their pupils' minds. And why, we might add, stop at Sunday School teachers? Is not the vast majority of Bible input the responsibility of parents as they read and pray with their children on a daily basis? There is a case here for reflecting upon how we do this, upon how we bring home to the minds of our own offspring the great pattern of God's consistent saving action through history.

Systematic theology

Third, the minister should have a solid grounding in systematic theology because the context of any given biblical text or narrative is theological as well as redemptive-historical. The doctrines of the trinity, of total depravity, of predestination, to name but three, need to be constantly before the minister's eyes as he reads the biblical text and as he moves from those texts to the sermon. Some evangelical church members, and even some ministers, decry 'systematic theology' as if it were some alien construct imposed on the text only to distort the Bible's own teaching; but such talk is arrant nonsense.

The Reformers were biblical exegetes par excellence, and yet they constantly brought 1500 years of doctrinal formulation to bear upon their exegesis. If systematic theology has been abused to produce exegetical distortion, that is the fault of the practitioners, not the discipline. What I suspect the pulpit critics of systematic theology more often mean is that the theological problem they face in the text is beyond their mental powers, and they are hoping to excuse their lack of hard-headed theological thinking in a manner which makes them appear more, not less, biblical. Better, apparently, to offer the congregation incoherence and confusion than draw upon the theological heritage of the church. Such superficiality has no place in an evangelical pulpit.

Here again, there is a case for saying that what is good for the ministerial goose is good for the congregational gander. Are not all Christians theologians? Do not all speak of God at some level? There is a need, then, for all to be schooled in the rudiments of systematic theology. We should remember how catechising has functioned in church history. We may smile at it today as being somewhat old-fashioned and quaint, but it did aim to give children and older church members a sound grasp of the full sweep of biblical teaching. In fact, in terms of his own ministry Richard Baxter considered it to be second in importance only to preaching. I am not saying we should necessarily return to catechising in the old form—that may well not be appropriate. What I am saying is that, if we do not, we should still be seeking for ways of achieving the catechetical aims which our forebears had in terms of educating for basic biblical and theological literacy. The more theology our people know, the more they will appreciate the value of the Bible and the more theology they will be able to find there.

Appropriate training

Ministerial training that is faithful to Reformation principles, then, gives due weight to the inspired text of the Bible by its emphasis on biblical languages, its attention to the unity of God's purposes in biblical history, and its commitment to the unified picture of God which is given in and through the Bible. Only once these things have been given centre stage, can other things be considered as part of the training curriculum. Indeed, the other essential aspects of ministerial training, such as homiletics, should be profoundly shaped by what goes on in these three, for they should be above all concerned with how the knowledge gained thereby can be put to best use in the sermon form. Other aspects of the curriculum which have no relation to this central Word focus, such as the present fad of pastoral psychology, can and perhaps should be dispensed with. The minister's task is primarily to preach the Word, not to offer therapy; there are professionals who can do that, and do it much better; let the preacher concentrate on that to which he has been called.

Ability

Some may object at this point that I am presenting a picture of the minister which will really restrict the calling to those of intellectual ability. To an extent, that is true. While I would not want to make intellectual gifts an absolute prerequisite of ministry, it would seem to me that the minister must in general possess certain skills, such as those outlined above, in order to fulfil his task competently. When we consider for a moment that the intellectual health of the church depends to a large extent upon the intellectual vigour of its sermons, the skills of the minister in terms of languages, exegesis, and theology are clearly of great significance. Certainly it would never have occurred to the Reformers that the minister should not have received the best education possible; and whatever else it may have meant, their notion of the perspicuity of Scripture did not mean that they considered Scripture's message to be so superficial that it could be grasped in all its length, depth and breadth by those who simply picked up a Bible translation and started reading. No, education for ministers was crucial, as the founding of the Academy of Geneva in 1559 demonstrates; and as, for example, the presbyterian tradition in Scotland has always sought to maintain.

We live in a profoundly anti-intellectual culture and at a time when pragmatism in its various forms reigns pretty much supreme. We must beware that when we are tempted to decry the traditional concept of ministerial training, we do not do so for reasons which arise from an unconscious aping of the surrounding culture. Theology is a difficult subject; and ensuring that the complexities of the Bible are accessible to the lay person makes the minister's task even harder. There is a need, therefore, for ministers with both the ability and the training to accomplish the task in a sound and God-glorifying manner. These are the qualities of good ministerial training and, one should perhaps add, the priorities when a church is looking to call a minister.

THE MINISTER'S TASK

A feeling of call to the ministry and good theological training are not, however, all that makes a good, Word-based minister or ministry. Now I am afraid I must confess at this point that I belong to the old reactionary tendency which regards the man who cannot preach in an interesting and informative manner as simply not called to the preaching ministry. If a man mounts a pulpit and cannot set his people's heart on fire for the Bible, then he had better not step into the pulpit at all, for to put Christians off hearing and reading the Word of God has to be one of the most serious acts one can commit.

An infectious enthusiasm

My views on this matter arise from my belief that the minister's task is not simply to present an accurate exposition of a set passage or verse; it is also to encourage and enable his people to go away and read the Bible for themselves in a responsible and intelligent manner. As he preaches the Bible week by week, he is not simply bringing home the message of salvation on a Sunday but is equipping his people for reading, studying and appropriating that message of salvation during the week. After all, at the heart of the Reformation was the emphasis upon lay possession and reading of the Scriptures. This was not, as is popularly misconstrued, a way of saying that every individual had the right to claim that whatever interpretation they cared to put on the passage was the correct one or equally valid with any other (the way in which this often seems to play out in practice); rather, it was an acknowledgment that every one had the responsibility to read the Bible for themselves in order that each should come to grasp the reality of God's grace in Jesus Christ. The preaching ministry, on one level, was therefore a means to facilitate precisely such responsible handling of the Bible.

This should be an underlying concern in ministry today. We live in a day when ignorance of the most basic stories of the Bible, let alone its overall structure, is rife, even among evangelical Christians. One part of the minister's brief, therefore, is to demonstrate to his people how to read, interpret and apply the Bible in a responsible manner. All this can be learned at Bible college; but what cannot be learned is that surpassing love for the Lord Jesus Christ which flows over into an enthusiasm for the Bible and its teachings which, when coming from the pulpit and driven home by the Holy Spirit, is little short of infectious. If the minister cannot himself show that reading the Bible is a vital and inspiring thing, then he can hardly complain if his people follow his lead in finding it dull and irrelevant. Only as Christ is glorified through the preaching of the Bible week by week will people come to see that Bible Christianity is Christ Christianity; only then will they realise that the Bible is the only thing through which they find access to such a Saviour.

The central issue

In conclusion, I must say that I think the centrality of the Word as Word is probably the key battle ground in evangelical church life today. We are all used to those who deny the plenary inspiration and authority of Scripture; but the debates have become far more wide-ranging and damaging even than that. Is salvation only by Christ? Is redemption through Christ only revealed in the Scriptures? Can the gospel be communicated in a non-verbal way in a manner which is at all meaningful? These are all challenges which the trendy gurus of postevangelicalism are throwing at the traditional evangelical church and which derive from a failure to see the Bible as God's Word, a Word spoken, as Francis Schaeffer would say, by the God who is there and who is not silent. The collapse in evangelical doctrinal consensus is intimately related to the collapse in the understanding of, and role assigned to, Scripture as God's Word spoken within the church.

For all the claims, however, that society is now 'too visual' for old-style word-centred religion, and that a book-based evangelicalism runs the risk of becoming a ghetto of middle class, cerebral bookworms with nothing to say to the Generation Xers, there is one embarrassing fact that the new gurus need to face: God gave us a book, full of words, as the basic means of giving us access to his revelation. The gospel is therefore ineradicably verbal and the Bible must remain non-negotiably at the centre of church policy, ministerial training and family life. Not to do so is to leave ourselves vulnerable to every puff of heretical wind that the gurus blow in our direction. It is also to set ourselves above what God himself has laid out for us.

Command, promise, Messiah—the basic terms of the Bible's message are ineradicably verbal and cannot be communicated in isolation from words. Bin the words and whatever else you are left with; it is not Christianity, biblical, historical or otherwise. We do need to think about how such a word-based religion can be communicated in this day and generation; we do need to avoid at all costs becoming a middle-class ghetto for frustrated academics. But we also need to be faithful to the Bible's own form and matter, both of which involve words at their very centre. Let us not despair: the Word is not just the Word; it is the Word of, in, and through the Spirit. It is powerful in its very essence. Our task is ultimately to communicate it; the power of the communication resides in God alone. Let us remember the words of Isaiah and concentrate not so much upon technique as upon the moral attitude we should adopt:

This is the one I esteem: he who is humble and contrite in spirit, and trembles at my word. (Isa. 66:2).

4 BLESSED ASSURANCE

It was the English Reformer, John Bradford, who declared that the basic difference between Reformation Protestantism and contemporary Catholicism was the fact that the former believed that assurance was a normative part of Christian faith and that the possession of assurance should therefore be part of every believer's experience. In saying this, he consciously touched upon two very deep insights of the Reformers: the doctrine of justification by grace through faith, the means by which the salvation wrought in Christ was appropriated by the believer; and the election of individuals to salvation by God's sovereign and gracious choice, the framework within which justification by grace operated. Both strands of Reformation thinking were indissolubly connected; and both pointed to, and gave firm grounds for, assurance of God's favour towards sinners.

A REFORMATION BEDROCK

Bradford's comments stand in basic continuity with concerns evident in Reformation theology from its very inception. The story of Martin Luther's struggles with his own sinfulness, and the failure of medieval theology to help him in that struggle, is well known.

Luther's experience

As a monk, Luther had wrestled long and hard with the fact that he was not good enough to stand in God's presence: he had driven himself to the limits of human endurance in his attempts to crush his sinfulness and make himself righteous. In his quest to purge out all sin, he had driven his confessor almost to the point of distraction with his pathological attention to the details of his life; and he had found that the medieval notion that God would be gracious to those who did their best to be a source not of comfort but of further agony— for how could he ever be sure that he had indeed done his best? If that was the gospel, then it was far from being good news—rather, for Luther, it was further bad news, meaning that not just the law, but even the gospel acted as a basis for accusation and condemnation for those serious about the condition of their soul.

The conclusion of the story is equally well known. While wrestling with Romans 1:17, Luther came to understand that God's righteousness is not something akin to some objective standard by which humans are weighed in the balance and found wanting; it is rather a gift of God whereby the individual is accounted righteous before God. It is, in other words, to be found in the great saving purpose of God as demonstrated in Christ on the cross at Calvary. There it is that the gospel is to be seen in all its glory, in the humiliation and suffering of the God who became man in the person of Jesus of Nazareth. Luther's real insight was to realise that the gospel was not about looking inward to self in order to find a basis for God's acceptance, but about looking outwards to the great saving act of God in Christ as the only way in which the sinner might come to the Father.

A revolutionary revelation

What Luther was struggling with was the medieval commonplace that assurance was not to be the normal state of the Christian. In the Middle Ages, the Church taught that no one could have assurance of salvation other than those especially blessed individuals who had received a special revelation from God that they were of the elect; and, indeed, the medieval understanding of grace, with its emphasis upon the Church as a corporate, sacramental body, had little need of individual assurance within its system. The result was that when a man such as Luther came along, burning within his soul to be assured that he, though a sinner, could yet stand as righteous before a holy God, the medieval system simply did not have the resources to help him, and he was driven back to the Bible and forced to wrestle anew with the text of Scripture in order to find an answer. And the answer that Luther found, that the Christian can have assurance because salvation depends upon the action of God, not upon the co-operation of God and humanity, set the agenda for subsequent Protestant thought.

In the wake of Luther's great insight, then, assurance of God's favour became a central part of Protestant thinking, as we see in the comment of John Bradford, where the major differences between Protestantism and Catholicism are seen to culminate or to focus on this one issue. Indeed, in Calvin's definition of faith as a sure and certain knowledge of God's favour we see that the same note is struck again. Furthermore, while the Westminster Confession of Faith, chapter 18, paragraph 3, allows for assurance not being so attached to faith that a true believer may not have the latter without the former, yet assurance remains the state to which all should not only aspire, but also expect in the ordinary course of a principled Christian life.

Its significance

This emphasis on assurance is important because such assurance of faith functions in Reformation Protestantism as far more than just a sedative for disturbed consciences. For example, in its emphasis upon God's sovereign and gracious action, it draws attention to the kind of unconditionally loving and merciful God which the Reformation sought to put on centre stage. Further, in the connection which the Reformers drew between God's free grace and the response of love in the human heart, assurance became the foundation for Christian activity: it is because we know that God loves us that we respond in love to him; and it is because he loves us and gives himself for us unconditionally that we love our neighbours and give ourselves unconditionally to them. Thus, the whole of the Christian life is profoundly shaped by the one brilliant insight: that God's love is unconditional and total, that it brings us salvation as a gift, and that, most amazing of all, we can know this salvation for certain for ourselves.

The biblical revelation

That assurance was important to the Reformers is no less than we should expect from those who sought to place God's grace at the centre of the church's life. This is how it should be. The Reformation God is the biblical God of grace, the God of sovereign grace, who has revealed himself throughout the sacred history of the Scriptures as the one who has promised to be gracious to his people and who has, time and again, honoured that promise. From the covenant with Abraham, through the stories of Isaac, Jacob, Joseph, Moses, David, Solomon, Hezekiah, down to Mary, Elizabeth and Simeon, God was not just faithful to his promise of grace but demonstrated himself so to be in clear, unequivocal fashion. Then, in Christ we have the supreme demonstration of God's trustworthiness and commitment—God himself coming voluntarily to dwell as a human among other humans, and dying on a cross so that we might have life and have it to the full.

The Bible is a book that speaks of nothing so much as God's clear and open trustworthiness in the matter of his gracious and merciful dealings with humanity. Thus, it was inevitable that a movement which took God's grace so seriously inevitably placed Christ and the Bible at the centre of its reforming programme, and underscored the fact that God does not just save, but gives us firm and secure grounds for knowing that he has so acted: the sacred history, the life and work of Jesus Christ, and the inspired Bible which is the means by which, humanly speaking, we come to know and understand these things.

The question now arises: how can we be faithful in contemporary church life to this basic insight concerning the importance of assurance? It is clear, after all, that any kind of theology we may develop in our churches, no matter how Protestant it may appear in terms of its words and general content, will yet fail to be truly Protestant, truly continuous with the thought represented by, say, John Bradford, if it does not place assurance somewhere near the centre of its concerns. Before we can answer the question, however, we need to reflect upon the church situation which we see around us at the present time to understand, first, whether problems associated with assurance are afflicting the church today, and of what kind they are; and, secondly, exactly what proper, biblical assurance means.

THE EVANGELICAL CHURCH TODAY

I suspect we can, with just a little over-simplification, divide the contemporary evangelical world up into two camps: the legalists, and the emotional high-fliers. Perhaps there are more categories than this; perhaps, in some cases, the categories are not discrete and flow into each other; but, broadly conceived, I think this division provides us with a useful model for analysing the contemporary scene.

Legalists

The first group, the legalists, are perhaps most common in, though by no means confined to, certain branches of Highland Presbyterianism and certain strands within the Strict Baptist tradition. To this group, the Westminster Confession's statement that assurance can sometimes elude the true believer for some considerable time is less of a concession to exceptional pastoral realities and more of a normative statement about the standard Christian life. The bottom line in such circles is an emphasis upon the need for either deep Christian experiences or a certain period of 'godly walking before the Lord' as a necessary pre-requisite for full acceptance within the church community, either by baptism or participation in the Lord's Supper.

I have many friends and relatives in the Highland Presbyterian tradition and am myself a member of the Free Church of Scotland, a denomination which, at least in the west of Scotland and the Hebrides, is identified in many minds with precisely the kind of piety to which I am now referring. In the past, many would not go forward to communion (the means in this tradition of making public profession of faith) until years after they had actually turned to Christ in repentance and faith. Some genuinely lacked assurance for a long period of time; others lacked the courage that a profession of faith requires in a close-knit community where lives are scrutinised by neighbours in intimate detail for signs of genuine faith; still others perversely made lack of assurance into a means of self-righteousness, looking down on others who were younger yet who went forward to communion as presumptuous and as lacking a deep knowledge of their own sinfulness—perversely, then, lack of assurance becomes itself a sign of election! In my experience, these people never seemed to think that such an attitude demonstrated on their part not a deeper knowledge of their own sin but a shallower knowledge of Christ.

Whatever the reason for any individual believer's failure to make public profession of faith in such a context, two general observations can be made at this point. First, the delay between conversion and public profession to which such situations witness is possible only within a church culture which accepts that such a pattern is legitimate, if not actually normative. The problem is not therefore simply one of various individuals struggling with making public profession; it is one of a community which has created a social and theological context, a framework of values and expectations, which allows such a phenomenon to persist.

Second, however Protestant such a group might like to think itself to be, however much it uses the language and rhetoric of the Reformation, however much it pays lip-service to the names and the deeds of the Reformers, it is clearly a long way from the Protestantism envisaged by John Bradford and his contemporaries; and, indeed, it would seem closer on this issue to the very Catholicism which Bradford and company were so keen to repudiate. It is, after all, not enough to have an intellectual commitment to the truth of Reformation doctrine if one wishes to lay claim to the Reformers' legacy; one must also use or apply their doctrine in a manner continuous with the way in which they themselves used it. After all, one might believe in the power of penicillin to heal, but if one uses it, albeit accidentally and out of ignorance, to kill or to harm, one places oneself outside of the tradition of accepted medical practice.

The emotional high-fliers

While the legalists tend to end up stressing subjective factors—experience, godliness, etc—as the basis for assurance and thus membership of the church, the more prevalent problem today in British evangelicalism is, I suspect, that of those who tend to understand assurance as feeling good or happy about oneself as a Christian, and who thus create a view of the Christian life conceived of in emotional terms. Now I certainly do not want to eliminate the emotional element from Christian assurance; all I would plead for is that we have the good sense to realise that Christian joy and Christian peace are rooted in factors which go much deeper than personal experience and are thus different in many ways from the usual human understanding of such emotions.

We are generally joyful when something good happens to us; we are at peace when some burden or problem affecting us or our loved one is removed. Of course, Christian joy and peace are not less than these: forgiveness of sins and assurance of God's favour both qualify as things which we experience and they call forth from our hearts feelings of joy and peace; but they are also, to use the technical term, eschatological experiences. Put simply, that means they are things which we know by faith are true now, but which we will not fully experience and know directly, as it were by sight, until the very end of time. Until then, the world labours under the burden of human wickedness which has spoiled its original perfection; we groan inwardly with the torments of our own sinfulness, and life can never be fully satisfactory to us. There is an element in Christian faith which must always be dissatisfied with and protest against the present status quo. After all, what is faith but belief in a promise; and what is belief in a promise other than something which embodies within it hope for the future and dissatisfaction with the present. This is of the essence of the biblical narrative, whether in the stories of Abraham's wanderings, the Exodus from Egypt or the fasting (that ancient sign of protest) of the prophetess Anna as she waited for the salvation of Israel.

A piety, therefore, which roots itself in assurance as immediate joy and total satisfaction in the present represents, again to use a technical phrase, an over-realised eschatology. That is to say, it represents a failure to realise that the kingdom of God, while inaugurated now, is not yet consummated, and that assurance that God is who he is must not therefore be tied to a theology which emphasises the relentless present triumph of the gospel, either in our own individual lives or in the wider church or in the world as a whole. To make this mistake is to invite disaster, for as soon as things do not go our way or, when we come down from our emotional highs, we will find that our assurance of God's favour will disappear. We must remember rather that God's saving purposes have been revealed and accomplished in Christ, but we must wait for the end of time to see and experience the unmitigated joy which his final triumph will bring about

THE BASIS FOR ASSURANCE

In a strange way, both of these excesses, the intro-spective legalism which devalues assurance and the joyful triumphalism which virtually denies that the believer can or should ever feel less than a full emotional high, are symptomatic of the same thing: an obsession with the experience of the believer as the basis for assurance. Both the introspective legalist and the joyful triumphalist look to their feelings for signs that they are elect or saved; and both effectively identify assurance with the subjective work of God in their own lives. One has only to think of the role played in both traditions by personal testimonies—what God has done for me and in me—to see the truth of this assertion. Not that there is anything wrong with personal testimonies—providing they are kept in their proper perspective, within the larger framework of God's saving dealings with his people. Nevertheless, it is this emphasis upon personal experience as of the essence of assurance which, I would suggest, is where both streams of evangelicalism deviate from the basic emphases of the Reformers.

The Reformers

For the Reformers, assurance arose from the perception that God was both trustworthy and that his promise to save was, in an important sense, unconditional. When God gave his covenant promise to Abraham, the accent was not on the mutual relationship of God and humanity, such that God would act to save if humanity played its part in return. Not at all. The accent was rather on the promise: that God was gracious and intended to save graciously, that election to salvation was not in the power of men and women but resided solely in the hands of God alone. Throughout biblical history God had demonstrated again and again that he, the God who promised, was trustworthy, in the way that time and time again he preserved his people and the messianic line, often in the face of great apostasy, until that moment in Bethlehem when the Christ child was born. Then, of course, in the person of Jesus Christ, God brought to ultimate fulfilment his promise of grace—not with the aid of humans but, as the virgin birth itself reminds us, solely by an unconditional act of his own grace. This point, that God is trustworthy, and that we know that he is trustworthy because of the way he has acted throughout biblical history, especially as it culminates in Christ, is the foundation for assurance, and not yours or my personal experience or emotional highs.

Luther

What we find when we turn to look at the works of, say Luther, is an overwhelming emphasis upon the objective works of God, specifically in this case the incarnation. Luther knows that he faces a gracious God because God became human in Bethlehem at a given point in time. Manifested in the flesh of Christ is God as gracious towards sinners. That is why Luther can feel assured and why he can rejoice in God's favour, like a prisoner released from prison. His assurance is rooted in the historical deeds of God as described in the Bible, as spoken forth in preaching and as displayed in baptism and the Lord's Supper. Sure, Luther talks about the emotional highs and lows of being a Christian, but his assurance is never rooted in these. If it were, his delight in the Lord might easily ebb and flow with the amount of sleep he had at night, the balance of his diet or the ups and downs of Wittenberg politics.

This truth is highlighted by Luther's comment on Jesus Christ in his *Small Catechism*:

> I believe that Jesus Christ, true God, begotten of the Father from eternity, and also true man, born of the Virgin Mary, is my Lord; who has redeemed me, a lost and condemned man, secured and delivered me from all sins, from death, and from the power of the devil, not with gold or silver, but with his holy, precious blood, and with his innocent sufferings and death; in order that I might be his own, live under him in everlasting righteousness, innocence, and blessedness, even as he is risen from the dead and lives and reigns forever. This is most certainly true. (Taken from Schaff's *Creeds of Christendom*)

Thus, it is God's action in Christ which both secures salvation and undergirds the Christian's subsequent life. Who can read Luther's references to his own religious experiences without seeing that it is his great grasp of what Christ has done for the church which secures his assurance and drives his Christian confidence?

Calvin

The same is true for Calvin. With Calvin, of course, we have much less knowledge of his personal experience of the Christian life than we have of Luther. Calvin, true to the portraits we have of him, is serious, private and reticent about the intimate details of his own religious life. Nevertheless, here is a man for whom assurance of God's favour is of the essence of the Christian faith. Now while some of us might feel that he over-stated the relationship between faith and assurance as a reaction to medieval excesses in the opposite direction (and I confess myself to prefer the emphases of the Westminster Confession on this issue), it is clear that he rooted his confident assurance in God in the great saving acts of God in history, supremely that of Jesus Christ. Listen, for example, to how he describes the gospel at the start of *The Harmony of the Evangelists*:

> The Gospel is a public exhibition of the Son of God manifested in the flesh to deliver a ruined world, and to restore men from death to life. It is justly called a good and joyful message, for it contains perfect happiness.

In what, then, does perfect happiness consist? It consists in seeing Christ set forth, in seeing what he has done for us. That is where our assurance must be rooted.

The Bible

Now, what the Reformers saw here is actually little more than the pattern of the Bible itself. If we look in the Bible for those points where assurance of God's favour was looked for, what do we find? Time and again we see believers referred back to the great deeds of God in history as the basis for assurance, to those acts by which God not only revealed himself as the one who saves but also as the one who is fundamentally true to his promise of grace as given to the patriarchs. It is neither their own experiences nor their emotional states which provide them with assurance: the rock upon which their confidence and joy are built is the constant recollection of how faithful God has been to his people throughout history.

ASSURANCE TODAY: THE CONTENT OF PREACHING

This brings us once again to the question of how this basic and important insight of the Reformers can be applied within the church today. In this context, the first point I would like to make concerns the content of the preaching we hear from our pulpits on a week-by-week basis. As I argued in the first chapter, preaching is essential in setting the tone of the church's life and expectation, and so it is here that reformation needs to begin.

Both of the caricatures I drew earlier—the legalists and the emotional high-fliers—are in part the result of faulty preaching. Now I know that many other factors also influence such groups. We should be aware at the start that there really is no such thing as 'a problem with assurance', as if there were only one cause of the various problems we see around us. There are many reasons why different people suffer from problems related to assurance, and, to an extent, these must be dealt with on the level of particular individuals and instances. In addition, the larger framework within which these problems occur is also significant: wider community expectations, personal histories, etc, can all help to shape and define the problem—and the church leadership can rarely deal with these things in a simple and straightforward manner. Community expectations, for example, can take years to change; but part of effecting that change is to make sure that the message coming from the pulpit is sound and balanced. If that is done, then we can surely pray that God in his grace will use this to start effecting the necessary changes in those hidden yet powerful social forces which shape the piety and attitudes of a congregation as a whole.

So what constitutes such preaching? In answer to this question, I would like to propose three characteristics: it is to centre on God; it is to centre on biblical history; and it is to centre on Christ. In saying this, I virtually repeat myself, as each of these is simply a way of saying that such preaching should be fundamentally biblical. Yet each phrase also captures something of a different nuance which I wish to highlight.

Centred on God

First, such preaching is to centre on God. Both the introspective legalists and the emotional high-fliers, as I have said, make the basic mistake of placing their emphasis ultimately on their own experience. Their religion, whatever the rhetoric of godly piety with which they may surround it, is essentially a human-centred one where they and their experiences are the things about which they are most concerned. The way to counter this is surely to draw the minds of the people away from themselves and on to the God of the Bible, and that is done by making sure that when the Bible is preached, it is preached as God's story.

Look at the examples of sermons in the New Testament or at the letters written by Paul and others: the focus is invariably upon God and God's actions, with the practical human application, if and when it comes, arising precisely out of the previous arguments concerning God. In Philippians, it is because God the Son, though equal with God the Father, humbled himself and took on the status of a servant that believers should look to the interests of others and give themselves in unconditional service to them. In Ephesians, it is because God chose and predestined believers in love before the foundation of the world that they should strive for unity in the body. At no point is the focus on individuals or individual experience as the basis for talking about God or making sense of God. Quite the reverse: God's actions provide the framework by which the believer's life is to be understood and regulated.

God's saving activity in the Bible story

From this flows the second point: preaching is to place biblical history high on its agenda. The pattern throughout the Bible is to root knowledge of who God is and of how he acts in the knowledge of the great saving acts of God in history. The Exodus from Egypt is, of course, the greatest example of this kind of action, whereby God frees his people from bondage in Egypt to bring them back to the land of Canaan. In the recitation of these deeds, in their exposition in sermons week by week, believers are reminded time and time again that God is a gracious God and a trustworthy

God, that he does not abandon his people and that his arm is not shortened so that he cannot save.

Now many will probably say that this is what they do already, and they may well be correct, but it is worth pondering exactly how the biblical histories are preached to see whether the accent really is upon the God who saves and not upon the people whom he uses. Take, for example, the stories in the Book of Daniel concerning the young men at the Babylonian court. How often these are preached as paradigms which we are to follow: like the men in the dispute over food, we are not to compromise with the world around us; like the trio who refuse to worship the statue, we are not to worship the false gods of this world; like Daniel in the lions' den, we are to obey God rather than men. Dare to be a Daniel is, I suspect, a title that has been used on more than one occasion when preaching from this book. And yet, is this truly God-centred preaching? Or does it actually place humanity, rather than God, at the centre of the story?

My own view would be that the primary purpose of these stories is to tell us something about the gracious and preserving power of God during the time of the Exile, that the stories are more about divine grace than about human determination. One of the things that is so remarkable about Calvin's exegesis is that, while there is always solid application, the Bible is read above all as the story of God's grace not human activity: that is a Reformation emphasis; that is an emphasis which surely goes some way to correcting the imbalances that produce a distorted emphasis upon human experience; and that is something which preachers today can ill afford to miss.

Preaching is not about pious platitudes; it is about God and his saving, sovereign grace. And practical applications and reflections upon human experience grow out of this; they do not feed into it. The believer who is only told about Daniel as a pattern for the godliness he or she must achieve is surely doomed to introspection and despair; the believer who is told about how God preserved Daniel from the mouths of the lions is surely more likely to be encouraged to trust God despite his or her own feelings of weakness and inadequacy.

Culminating in Christ

This, then, leads inevitably to the third point: preaching is to be Christ-centred. Christ is the culmination of biblical history; and if in the proverb, all roads lead to Rome, then in the Bible, all roads lead to Christ. Luther, for all the problems that his understanding of Christ contained, really did hit the nail on the head when he found the answer to his problem in the person of the Lord Jesus Christ, for it is in Christ that we see the grace of God most fully and perfectly displayed. As we grasp him in faith, we stand before God not as sinners but as those clothed with a new and glorious righteousness. Indeed, assurance was such an important aspect of Reformation theology precisely because the Reformers placed Christ and the work which God accomplished in and through him right at the very centre of their theological programme.

Thus, it is crucial that, if our churches are to be filled with people who enjoy a proper and God-centred assurance, our pulpits should ring out week after week with the news that God was in Christ reconciling the world to himself. It is not enough to exegete the chosen text in a manner which is grammatically and syntactically correct; it is not enough to send the congregation home with some blessed thought hung on the hook of a biblical phrase; it is not even enough to derive some pious application from the text which will prove useful for others in the coming week; no, they need to be given Christ. No matter where in the Bible preachers are preaching from, if they truly believe that the Bible tells one story, if they truly believe that God's promise of grace is fulfilled in Christ, and if they truly wish to encourage proper Christian joy, assurance and devotion among their people, they will end up by giving them Christ. This Christ-centred focus is fundamental to the Reformers' preaching as it is to their understanding of the gospel; and, to the extent that this truly reflects the teaching of the Bible itself, to that extent it should be fundamental to all preaching.

This, of course, presupposes that it is biblical history that is being preached and taught. We need to avoid at all costs the idea that Christ is who he is primarily because of what he does for us as individuals. Now, do not misinterpret me here—I am not saying that what Christ does for us is not important. Rather, I am saying that we must remember—and then teach—that Christ is who he is because of the place he occupies in the biblical history of redemption. A Christ who is not understood within the context of the great biblical narrative and thus within the context of the great biblical covenants is a Christ without theological or historical identity. It is not possible to assure people that God is gracious to them in Christ if they have only the vaguest notions about Christ's identity, or, even worse, if they only know who he is in relation to their own experience.

It is no good telling the bereaved mother that Christ still loves and cares for her if she has only been taught to think of Christ in terms of how he works on her own feelings and in her own experiences. She needs to be able to see that God is much greater than her experience of him; she needs to know that, whatever her current feelings of anguish and despair, God is trustworthy and loving; and she needs to know that assurance is not necessarily about emotional highs but about knowing that God is faithful even though the whole world appears to be falling apart around her. Such will only be possible if the theological environment in which she lives and worships teaches her to understand Christ above all in terms of his historical work of redemption for the people of God; and that will only come about when the emphasis in preaching focuses not on ourselves but on the Christ of the Bible. Setting Christ above all in the context of biblical history rather than our own experience will promote a truly high understanding of Christ as Redeemer, and one that will ultimately be of more use than the Christ of Emotional Therapy that would seem today to be the preferred alternative in many circles, itself the result in part of our natural human tendency to place our needs rather than God's mighty acts of salvation at the centre of our theology.

ASSURANCE TODAY: THE LITURGY
In making preaching centre on God, on his saving acts and supremely on Christ, the preacher will automatically be creating an environment where the eyes of the congregation are drawn away from themselves, whether they be preoccupied with a morbid introspection or with an unhealthy excitement concerning their own experiences. Instead, they will have the opportunity to look to the objective, historical acts of God as the basis for their assurance and their joy, a much firmer foundation than any they might wish to build based on their own religious feelings. But, of course, this is only half of the story: not only should the preaching reflect these emphases, but the acts of corporate worship must do so as well.

Balanced
In the chapter on Christ, I spoke of the need for the church to take seriously the status of humanity as being redeemed yet not brought to final perfection.

This meant, I argued, that we should avoid a diet of unremittingly triumphalist sermons and hymns as these helped only to create a kind of macho evangelical culture of emotional joy and exuberance combined with absolutely no doubts about anything whatsoever. Such a culture is pastorally disastrous, evangelistically stunted, and, at the end of the day, simply represents a false understanding of what Christianity in the present is all about. I suggested, as an alternative, that a balanced approach to worship was more likely to be found in the emphases of the psalms, where we find not only joy, but also lament, and that both are therefore legitimate and important aspects of Christian worship.

Some might well be tempted to comment at this point that what I have been saying thus far in this lecture does not sit too easily with what I have said before. Does not lamentation involve a lack of assurance? If Christian worship is to give full rein to the great and glorious Reformation emphasis on assurance, then what place does lamentation have in Christian worship?

Looking to the past, present and future

My response to such a legitimate question is to focus upon exactly what Christian assurance is: it is, I believe, backward looking with regard to its foundation but forward looking in its orientation. In essence, assurance is being certain that God is who he says he is—and that is derived from our knowledge of his great saving acts throughout history as they culminate in Christ—and therefore being sure that he will bring us to glory, that he will complete that good work within us which he has started. We live in the present, at a time when we know that one day we will see God in glory but only see him now by faith. In the meantime, the world is a dark and hostile place; and our souls are in many ways still darkened and frequently tending to hostility towards God. Therefore, there will be times when, either because of external or because of internal factors, we do not see or feel God smiling upon us. At such times we can indeed lament our sorry condition. It is right and proper, and pastoral good sense, that we do so, because to do otherwise is to fool nobody, not even ourselves, and thus to store up trouble for later on; but as we do so, we should also remind ourselves that it is not what we feel now that determines our status, but who God was, is and always shall be. Thus, the lamentation should be set, as it almost invariably is in the psalms, within the context of God's larger redemptive acts and purposes.

God-centred

Thus, corporate worship, the hymns we sing, the words we say together, must not only be realistic with regards to the human condition; it must also take full account of God's mighty acts of salvation. Reformation liturgy captures this nicely. One has only to think of the role played by psalm singing in the Genevan Reformation, and of the metrical Psalter in the *Book of Common Prayer*, to see how central to Reformation worship were these great expressions of human emotion in the context of God's redeeming purposes. In addition, one can see from the importance of the Magnificat and the Nunc Dimittis in the *Book of Common Prayer* that for the Reformers worship was inextricably linked to God's redemptive acts in history as they culminated in Christ.

Now I am not one to get involved in the 'new' versus 'old' arguments that are so rampant in British Reformed evangelicalism at the moment and which not infrequently fracture fellowships and split churches. My impression of these debates is that often behind the theological rhetoric, the points at issue have more to do with style than with content. My interest here is not in style at all; and I am quite open to the possibility that my suggestions regarding worship can be as easily appropriated by a modern music or worship idiom as by the traditional ones with which I am more familiar. What I want to say is that the obsession in many quarters with hymns and choruses which never rise beyond the first person and never move outside of the sphere of describing personal experience (whether real or merely ideal) is basically unbiblical and that, however confident the rhetoric, they will not engender the kind of assurance which the Reformers saw the Bible as teaching. That is not to say that no hymn or chorus should speak of personal experience, or be constructed in the first person, but it is to say that when such experience is part of a hymn or a chorus, it should never be an end in itself or be the ultimate focus. If the hymn speaks of despair, then let it move on to reflect on the goodness of God in his acts of redemption and of his promise of coming glorification; if it speaks of joy, then let it not be some contentless joy which can give no grounds for its own existence; rather, let it be joy in some act of God; only then will the joy be truly stable and not just constructed on the emotional whim of the moment.

I am no fan of Anglican liturgy—or of formal liturgy in general for that matter—but two things I will say in its favour: in a liturgical setting, people rarely if ever speak nonsense in a church service; and in most liturgies of which I am aware, the focus is always ultimately upon God and his deeds, not human beings and their needs. And that is a good, sound, biblical emphasis.

Biblical assurance requires, first and foremost, that we know who God is; and that requires, secondly, knowing what he has done throughout history. This is what our preaching and our worship should reflect if we are to capture once again the true Reformation emphasis on assurance, that emphasis which should mark the dividing line between a biblical and joyful evangelicalism and the superficial froth or abject despair engendered by other versions of Christianity which may even claim the name evangelical and Protestant, and yet which lack that very thing which Reformers such as Bradford saw as essential to their project.

We have a gracious and trustworthy God; the Reformers reminded the world of that fact; let us place him once again at the centre of our lives and worship.

Christian Focus Publications
publishes books for all ages

Our mission statement –

STAYING FAITHFUL
In dependence upon God we seek to impact the world through literature faithful to His infallible Word, the Bible. Our aim is to ensure that the Lord Jesus Christ is presented as the only hope to obtain forgiveness of sin, live a useful life and look forward to heaven with Him.

REACHING OUT
Christ's last command requires us to reach out to our world with His gospel. We seek to help fulfill that by publishing books that point people towards Jesus and help them develop a Christ-like maturity. We aim to equip all levels of readers for life, work, ministry and mission.

Books in our adult range are published in three imprints:

Christian Focus contains popular works including biographies, commentaries, basic doctrine and Christian living. Our children's books are also published in this imprint.

Mentor focuses on books written at a level suitable for Bible College and seminary students, pastors, and other serious readers. The imprint includes commentaries, doctrinal studies, examination of current issues and church history.

Christian Heritage contains classic writings from the past.

Christian Focus Publications, Ltd
Geanies House, Fearn, Ross-shire,
IV20 1TW, Scotland, United Kingdom
www.christianfocus.com